LITERACY FOR DIVERSE LEARNERS:
Promoting Reading Growth at All Levels

Jerry L. Johns, *Editor*
Northern Illinois University

INTERNATIONAL READING ASSOCIATION
800 Barksdale Road   Newark, Delaware 19711

INTERNATIONAL READING ASSOCIATION

Library of Congress Cataloging in Publication Data
Main entry under title:

Literacy for diverse learners.

    Collection of papers drawn from the International
Reading Association's Denver convention of 1973.
    1. Reading—Congresses.   2. Negroes—Education—
Reading—Congresses.   I. Johns, Jerry L., ed.
II. International Reading Association.
LB1050.L498   428'.4   74-18059
ISBN 0-87207-471-4

CONTENTS

Acknowledgments   *iv*

Foreword   *v*

Introduction   *vii*

Dialect, Reading Materials, and the Culturally Diverse
Focus Questions   1

3   Black Dialect and Learning to Read   *Herbert D. Simons*

14   Relevant Content for the Black Elementary School Pupil   *Marian L. Vick*

23   Bilingualism, the School, and the Chicano: A Point of View   *David Conde*

Sources for Further Learning   28

Intelligence, Sex, and Reading Achievement
Focus Questions   29

31   Relationships Among IQ, Learning Ability, and Reading Achievement
    S. Jay Samuels and *Patricia R. Dahl*

39   Boys' Right to Read: Sex Factors in Learning to Read   *Richard Kolczynski*

Sources for Further Learning   46

Programs to Help Young Learners
Focus Questions   47

49   An Extended First and Second Grade Readiness Class: Content and Outcomes
    Sam Shohen

56   A Diagnostic-Prescriptive Reading Program   *Dorothy J. Gaither*

Sources for Further Learning   60

Programs to Help Disabled Readers
Focus Questions   61

63   A Remedial Reading Program Within a Communication Context
    Kathryn O'Connell and *Patricia Dew*

71   Coding: An Instructional Technique for Teaching Reading to Severely
    Disabled Readers   *Carl L. Rosen* and *Susan Tibbals*

78   Motivation Versus Cognitive Methods in Remedial Reading   *Clifford Carver*

Sources for Further Learning   84

Programs to Help Adult Learners
Focus Questions   85

87   Do Adult Literacy Programs Make A Difference?   *Edwin H. Smith* and
    McKinley Martin

93   Using Realia to Improve the Reading Skills of College Freshmen   *Frances Patai*

100   Teaching Educationally Disadvantaged Adults to Read: A Pilot Study
    Thomas R. Schnell

105   Promoting Literacy Through the Adult School Program
    Elinor Tripato Massoglia

Sources for Further Learning   120

ACKNOWLEDGMENTS

This volume is made possible through the efforts of a large number of professionals, many of whom are unknown to the editor. The anonymous members of the review committee responsible for the initial selection of papers are to be commended for the time and expertise they willingly devoted to this important, but frequently unrecognized task. Special thanks are also due to William K. Durr (Michigan State University) and Linda Lunt (Northern Illinois University) for reading the papers and offering useful suggestions and helpful criticisms. Finally, Faye R. Branca, Professional Publications Editor of the International Reading Association, deserves special thanks for her encouragement and wise counsel which helped to reduce the frustration in bringing this volume to fruition.

JLJ

FOREWORD

The International Reading Association is indebted to Jerry L. Johns for his selection and editing of this excellent collection of papers drawn from the Denver and other IRA conventions and to the authors who gave their time to report on the topic of literacy.

This book has many uses. Each section is prefaced by questions with which the authors deal, and concluded with a bibliography of articles and books of current importance published in the United States. Hence it is adaptable for independent study or as a text for teacher education courses. Instructors in other countries will add references from their own professional literature.

For teachers in the United States, the contents of this volume provide practical strategies and insights into the factors which must be considered in programs for illiterates, young or old.

For teachers in other countries, the benefits are the same except that when they read about ways of meeting the needs of black dialect speakers of English, they must think of parallels existing in their own settings and in relation to their national languages. When they read of problems of motivation for adults, they must think of the careers and environmental conditions of the adults in their societies.

What do you do after you finish reading such a book? Take notes? Bring new insights and altered approaches to your work? Lend the book to colleagues? Donate it to a library?

In the International Reading Association a colleague is someone who is trying to improve his role in the achievement of literacy. He is not necessarily in the classroom next door. He may live 12,000 miles away.

If you send him the book, he may see new possibilities in his own circumstances. His Council or Affiliate may produce a book of its own or write a report to one of the IRA journals. Someday that book or report may give you new insights into your situation and awareness of research findings useful to you.

Thus we generate more literacy for more diverse groups of learners. We learn from one another, and no one is only a giver or only a receiver. And we do this as professionals in the name of literacy.

Good reading, good progress.

Constance M. McCullough, *President*
International Reading Association
1974-1975

INTRODUCTION

Literacy, in the broadest sense, can be regarded as the mastery of our native language for the purposes of communication. Clearly, then, literacy involves skill in listening, speaking, and writing — as well as in reading. Although the fourteen papers in this volume focus on reading, the perceptive reader will not lose sight of the broader aspects and implications of the quest for literacy among diverse groups of learners. While the volume is not specifically addressed to a particular segment of the profession, a brief perusal of the contents will clearly indicate that teachers and researchers at all levels of reading instruction will find thought-provoking articles, ideas for classroom implementation, and suggestions for further research.

Each section begins with focus questions to aid the reader in acquiring the basic intent of the articles. The three papers in Section One deal with the issues of dialect, reading materials for black students, and bilingualism. Section Two includes two articles which explore the research on intelligence and sex factors as they relate to reading achievement; Section Three presents descriptions of two programs for preventing reading difficulties of young children; Section Four describes three programs that have been used with so-called "remedial" readers; and Section Five contains a welcomed focus on research and programs for a variety of adult learners. Also included at the end of each section is a selected bibliography of recently published and readily available books and articles for further learning.

All in all, the collection of papers in this volume should provide a basis for improving literacy among a wide range of learners, from beginners to adults. It is hoped that teachers, researchers, and other professionals will integrate the teaching and research strategies into their respective fields of endeavor.

JLJ

DIALECT, READING MATERIALS, AND THE CULTURALLY DIVERSE

FOCUS QUESTIONS

- What are the two points of view of the mismatch in dialect between the child's language and the school's language?
- What proposals have been made to reduce this mismatch?
- What factors have stimulated the trend toward so-called relevant materials for black children?
- What are some of the current materials for black children?
- What criteria should be employed in selecting relevant content for black children?
- Is bilingualism associated with low IQ scores?
- What has been the prevailing attitude of the school toward bilingualism?
- What are several characteristics that should permeate programs for bilinguals?

Reading and the Culturally Diverse

BLACK DIALECT AND LEARNING TO READ

Herbert D. Simons □ University of California

The upsurge of interest over the past decade on the question of the influence of black dialect on the acquisition of reading skills stems mainly from two observations. First, black children as a group are not learning to read (1); and second, black language differs from the language used in school and in particular from the language of the materials used in reading instruction. To be more specific, black children speak black dialect while the generally acceptable standard in the schools they attend is standard English. In effect, there is a discrepancy or mismatch between the child's language and the language of the school. On the basis of these observations it is widely assumed — explicitly or implicitly — by educators, linguists, psycholinguists, and others concerned with the reading instruction of black children that this mismatch is a major source of reading interference which is responsible for black children's lack of success in learning to read. It follows then, that it is necessary to reduce or eliminate this mismatch in order to improve the reading achievement of black children.

Mismatch in Dialect: Two Points of View

There are two points of view about the origin of the mismatch and ways to reduce it. The point of view held by most educators and many educational psychologists assumes that the child's language is deficient or defective and thus is the cause of the mismatch. This viewpoint has been labeled the deficit model. On the basis of this deficit assumption it becomes necessary to change the child's language so that it will conform to the language of the school. This usually involves some kind of attempt to develop the black dialect speaking child into a standard English speaker while at the same time eliminating completely his use of dialect (at least in school).

Another point of view recognizes that black language is a systematic and viable means of communication which is different from, but in no way inferior to, the standard English language that is acceptable in school. This point of view, which has been called the difference model, is held by some educators and educational psychologists as well as most linguists. Proponents of the difference model would require the schools to change in some ways to accommodate the child's language.

Thus, both the deficit and difference viewpoints accept the assumption that the mismatch between the child's language and the language used in school is a major factor in the reading problems of black children. They differ, however, in their proposed remedies. The deficit model would change the child's language while the difference model would change the school.

Proposals and Arguments for Reducing the Mismatch in Dialect

In recent years, three major proposals have been suggested for reducing the mismatch between the child's language and the school's language. The first proposal can be labeled the standard English (SE) approach in which attempts are made to either replace the child's dialect with SE or to provide him with SE as a second alternative dialect. This approach is motivated mainly, but not exclusively, by the deficit model and describes the dominant current practice. At the other extreme is a second proposal motivated by the difference model. This approach advocates teaching the black dialect (BD) speaker to read with reading materials written to conform to his dialect. This approach, which can be labeled the dialect reader approach, involves radical changes in the books used to teach reading. A third proposal, also motivated by the difference model, involves retaining existing reading materials but allowing BD speaking children to translate into their dialect when reading. This approach, as well as the dialect reader approach, would make no attempt to change the child's dialect, at least in the beginning stages of learning to read. Teachers would allow him to use dialect when reading.

The Standard English Approach. This approach has two versions. The first version describes current practice in which teachers unsystematically correct black children when they use dialect during reading instruction. The second version involves systematic practice with SE forms. This second version usually employs some sort of second language technique. The major argument for the SE approach is that it will reduce reading interference and presumably increase the reading performance of black children. There has not been any evidence presented to date that this will happen. One study (*8*), which tested the SE approach failed to increase significantly the use of SE and, consequently, reading did not improve. Perhaps one reason that attempts to teach SE have been unsuccessful is the heavy influence of peers on children's speech. This influence is so great that attempts to change dialects in school are difficult if not impossible. For this reason alone the SE approach appears doomed to failure. Another problem with the SE approach is that it may be seen by the child as a rejection of his language and, by implication, his culture. This perception may foster a negative attitude toward school which in turn will reduce motivation to learn to read. Finally, the proponents of this approach have confused speaking with reading and long term goals with short term goals. They believe that productive control of SE is necessary for adult success in society. They also believe that BD is an inferior form of communication; hence, the earlier BD is stamped out the better. These beliefs, both of which are questionable, motivate most educators and many black parents to support the SE approach even though it may be a very unpromising way of improving the reading performance of black children.

The SE approach appears to be a very unlikely method for helping black children to learn to read; in fact, the unsystematic version employed by many teachers probably interferes with a child's learning to read.

Dialect Readers. At the other end of the spectrum is the dialect reader approach which includes books written in dialect to be used during the early stages of reading instruction. It is assumed that written materials which approximate the speech of the child will be easier to learn to read than materials that are different from the reader's actual speech. Thus, by reducing the mismatch described earlier, dialect readers will improve reading. It is further argued that dialect readers will increase motivation to learn because the language is natural to black children. Research purports to show that in other countries children taught to read in the vernacular perform better than those taught with the standard language. Venezky (*13*), however, has questioned the validity of this research because of its methodological problems. There has been no evidence presented to substantiate the claim of their motivating effect. On the contrary, Mathewson (*5*) found that black primary grade children have a more negative attitude toward stories written in dialect than stories written in standard English.

There are studies by Ruddell (*7*) and Tatham (*12*) which provide indirect support for the claim that children will comprehend reading material written in dialect better than reading material written in SE. They found that white elementary school children comprehended material written with sentence patterns that occurred more frequently in their speech better than they did material composed of less frequent sentence patterns. If this finding could be replicated with black children, using materials written in their dialect, then the claim of better comprehension for dialect readers would be given strong support. However, this finding has not been replicated in studies of black children using dialect material. Studies by Schaaf (9), Sims (10), Johnson and Simons (3), and Mathewson (4) all failed to show that stories written in dialect were read better than parallel stories written in standard English. The type of remarkable improvement in reading that has been reported anecdotally by Stewart (11), for stories written in dialect, has evaporated in controlled experimentation.

It appears that none of the claims for dialect readers have been substantiated. Even if evidence 'to support the claims could be provided, there are other practical problems that raise barriers to the use of dialect readers in the schools. First, there is the problem of how close a match to the black children's dialect is possible in a set of reading books. Since the frequency of dialect features produced varies between individuals and is also influenced by social class, age, and the speech situation, it is not clear how much of a reduction of the mismatch can be attained with a given set of readers for a classroom full of black children. The problem is compounded in multiethnic classrooms. One would need more than one set of readers which vary in frequency of dialect features to attain even a rough approximation of children's speech. Printing different sets of readers with different frequencies of occurrence of dialect features would be expensive and would present problems in matching books to children. The logistic problems are formidable and it is not clear whether the gains in achievement would be worth the effort.

Another major obstacle to the use of dialect readers is the opposition of black parents and community groups. They object to dialect readers because, among other reasons, they view such materials as perpetuating and encouraging the use of dialect. They believe that it is necessary to eradicate this incorrect speech (which is what they think dialect is) in order to succeed in a predominantly white society. Because of this opposition, it is difficult to get even an experimental program using dialect readers adopted. It is important to change parents' attitudes and beliefs about dialect, but it is not clear that dialect readers should provide the battleground for this educational campaign.

In light of these obstacles, proposals for the use of dialect readers should be abandoned until strong evidence can be presented to show that they can make an important contribution to improving the reading performance of black children.

Dialect Rendition of Extant Materials. A third alternative for the handling of dialect in the reading instruction of black children has been proposed by Goodman (2). He suggests that existing reading materials which are written in standard English be retained but that the child be allowed to read the materials in his own dialect — that is, the child be allowed to translate into his own dialect when making oral responses. This proposal avoids some important disadvantages of the other alternatives. Since it recognizes the legitimacy of the child's language and makes no attempt to change it, the problem of rejecting the child's language inherent in the standard English approach is avoided. And, by not calling for materials written in dialect, Goodman's proposal avoids the practical problems with dialect readers previously discussed.

The Goodman proposal has no real disadvantages, except that it would require extensive changes in the way most teachers are handling dialect. This would involve extensive retraining of teachers. Surprisingly, there have been few, if any, research attempts to verify the Goodman proposal. This proposal is important, however, because it directs attention to what in all likelihood is the major source of reading interference for black children — the teacher's way of responding to black children when they use dialect during reading instruction.

Teacher Responses to Dialect and Reading Interference

The author believes that the teacher's interaction with the black dialect speaking child during reading instruction, rather than dialect per se, is a major source of reading interference. More specifically, it is the teacher's lack of knowledge of the rules of dialect and his attitude toward dialect which is a major source of reading interference.

The problem of how teachers handle dialect has been studied by Piestrup (6). She observed and tape recorded first grade teachers during the reading instruction of black children. She found differences in the way teachers responded to children's use of dialect and these differences were associated with differences in reading performance. The episodes of teacher-child interaction that Piestrup describes constitute the clearest evidence to date regarding the influence of teachers' ignorance of the rules of dialect and the resulting affect on children's reading. If the three examples discussed below are typical, they leave little doubt where the problem of dialect interference with the acquisition of reading skills lies.

The first example begins with a child (C_1) in a reading group reading the sentences, They call, "What is it?" "What is it?"

C_1 Dey . . .

T   Get your finger out of your mouth.

C_1 call . . .

T   Start again.

C_1 Dey call, what is it? What is it?

T   [asks a second child]

C_2 Dey.

C_1 Dat.

T   What is it?

C_2 Dat.

C_3 Dey.

C_4 [laughing]

C_1 Dey.

T   Look at my tongue. [between teeth]

C_1 They.

T   That's right. Say it again.

C_2 They.

T   They. OK. Pretty good. OK, Jimmy. (6:54-55)

In this episode the teacher demonstrates her ignorance of the difference between a reading error and a dialect difference. C_1's first response was correct for his dialect. The teacher, not recognizing that it was correct, asks C_1 to repeat it. This in effect tells C_1 and the other children that "Dey" is wrong. C_1 persists with the same answer because he doesn't know what else to say. He is not aware that it is the digraph part of the word that is wrong in the teacher's eyes. Probably out of frustration, C_1 then switches to a different word, "Dat," but maintains the dialect pronunciation of the interdental. When the teacher again questions these responses, the children are probably both confused and frustrated about what the teacher wants and about what the printed word is. C_1 finally goes back to his original response, but this still is not correct in the teacher's eyes and she proceeds to make the reading lesson into one of standard English pronunciation. The children then produce the correct response in SE and that satisfies the teacher. However, the children's reward is the not so subtle put down, "OK." What started out as a simple reading exercise that appeared to be well within the capabilities of the children turned into a lesson in standard English pronunciation. It is quite likely that the children have not increased their reading skills from this episode. In fact, they are probably more confused about reading and its function than when they started. In addition, they now may be more self-conscious of their speech during reading. All of this may slow their rate of reading and make them reluctant to respond in the future. It is likely that such episodes retard learning to read more than they advance it. The teacher is thoroughly confused about the difference between reading and speaking and the children are also probably confused about what they are expected to learn during reading instruction.

A second episode from Piestrup (6:63) points out further problems. The first part of the episode follows:

T   Who can give me a sentence with "win"?
C_1 A boy win a race.
T   A boy *win* a race?
C_2 I know teacher
C_3 I know teacher
T   Hm, that sounds
C_4 Teacher, I know one
T   . . . Can you say that a little better, so it sounds – I understand what you mean, but Erndalyn, what, how would you say that?
C_5 The win blew the hat off my frien' head.

The episode contains another example of teacher ignorance of the rules of black dialect. Since *win* and *wind* are homophones in dialect, the original question is ambiguous. A sentence using either word would be correct. However, when C_1 provides a sentence with *win* used properly in his dialect, the teacher in effect tells him he is wrong. He is wrong in the teacher's eyes for not producing a standard English sentence. That this is the problem is not clear to the children. C_5 sees the problem is use of the wrong word. And thus C_5 provides a sentence with the word *wind*, still in dialect. In this episode so far, the only right answers are those that are in standard English form. However, the children don't know that and are focusing on the content of the question rather than the form of the answer. When they give the right answer in dialect they are corrected. In response, however, they change the answer, not their dialect. It is easy to see how children can become confused.

The teacher in this episode has heard some lectures on black dialect, but she has an imperfect understanding of its rules and how it should be handled in reading. The remainder of the episode below illustrates this point.

T	Okay, that's what "win" sounds like, huh. But this is the kind of "win" when we, when you beat somebody else, when you win a race, OK? The other word, I'll show you how it's spelled. What word is this, Erndalyn? [Teacher writes "win" and "wind"] OK? And this is the kind of win we're talking about. [Points to "win"] This has a . . . [Points to "wind"]
C	"d"
T	What's on the end
C_6	A silent "d"
T	A "d." It's hard to hear.
$C_{6,7}$	It's a silent "d."
T	Well, it's not really, really silent, but it's just really hard to hear. It's there. Sometimes we can say it so we can hear it. Can you hear the name of it? Did you hear the "d" then? And we usually, some times we usually don't say it, but it's there, so Erndalyn what does this, make a sentence with this kind of "win."

In the second part of the episode, the teacher realizes that she has been using a homophone in BD and she capitalizes on this information by pointing out that they are spelled differently. But she is ambivalent and fails to reinforce the children's insight that the *d* is silent. Her mention that it is hard to hear leaves the impression that there is something wrong with not pronouncing it. She could have capitalized on the children's insight with a discussion of silent letters and by pointing out other examples. The teacher's knowledge of BD, however, has allowed her to see the ambiguity of her original question and to correct some of the confusion. Unfortunately, she did not go far enough in using the children's insights.

Finally, a third example (6:93-94) shows a teacher focusing upon speech at the expense of reading.

T	Tell me the sound you hear at the beginning and the sound you hear at the end. [Teacher shows pictures]
Class	Ham, H — m
T	Who wants a hard one? Janet, I have a "ship"
C_1	It begin with a . . .
T	Begins with a, let's say it for her
Class	Ship
	. . .
T	[Shows picture of a pencil]
Class	Pencil
C_3	It begin with a "p"
T	It begins with a "p"

C$_3$ And it end with an "l"

T   [Shows a picture of meat]

Class Mea'

T   It's not me! It's hard to hear the end sound but you really have to listen for it. It ends with a "t" if you say it that way. If you don't say it that way it ends with an "e."

Here, again, the teacher is ignorant of the rules of dialect and doesn't distinguish reading from speaking. She is teaching SE pronunciation by making the children respond in SE. For *ship* and *pencil* the child gives the right answer; however, the teacher corrects the child for giving the right answer in a dialect sentence. This draws attention away from the lesson which is concerned with beginning and ending sounds and focuses instead on producing SE sentences. This is entirely unnecessary, given the purpose of the lesson, and may in fact be detrimental because it gives the children the added task of producing responses in SE. Concerning the pronunciation of *meat* in which the final consonant is often reduced or deleted in dialect, the teacher resorts to the SE approach by explaining that the *t* is supposed to be pronounced.

Reading exercises with final consonants are a problem for dialect speakers since a number of consonant clusters have their second member eliminated and single consonants are reduced or eliminated. A more appropriate strategy might be to eliminate final consonant exercises in which an oral response is required and replace them with exercises where an oral response is not required, as in a matching exercise. The heavy emphasis upon final sounds found in many phonics programs is of dubious importance for all children and has never received much empirical support from the research. With black dialect speaking children, exercises involving ending sounds of words might profitably be eliminated.

These examples have shown, with striking clarity, what appears to be a major source of the problems resulting from the dialect of black children. If the practices described here are at all widespread, then the source of reading interference for BD speaking children comes from:

1. Teacher ignorance of the rules of BD.

2. Teacher confusion concerning the difference between reading and speaking.

3. Negative teacher attitudes toward BD and the belief that only SE speech is acceptable in the classroom.

A Solution to Dialect

It appears that a major effort will have to be made to reeducate teachers in order to remove these sources of interference. This is a formidable task because it involves not only providing information about dialect and the relationship of dialect to reading but also changing attitudes toward dialect. It requires 1) changes in the curricula of teacher training institutions to include courses in social class dialects and reading, 2) extensive inservice training for teachers in ghetto schools, 3) adaptation of published reading programs and materials to avoid encouraging the types of practice exercises described earlier.

All of these recommendations are directed at the elimination of negative practices; however, the elimination of these practices may not be enough. In all likelihood it will be necessary to develop new forms of reading instruction that take advantage of the function of language in black culture and of the verbal skills of black children. This requires a much firmer research knowledge of the reading acquisition process, the sociolinguistic situation that the classroom presents to black children, and its effects on their learning and motivation. A major research effort is required to provide this information. This research hopefully will lead to more effective and creative ways of teaching black children to read.

REFERENCES

1. Coleman, J. et al. *Equality of Educational Opportunity.* Washington, D.C.: U. S. Office of Education, 1966.
2. Goodman, K. "Dialect Barriers to Reading Comprehension," in J. Baratz and R. Shuy (Eds.), *Teaching Black Children to Read.* Washington, D.C.: Center for Applied Linguistics, 1969, 14-28.
3. Johnson, K., and H. Simons. *Black Children's Reading of Dialect and Standard Texts.* Washington, D.C.: U. S. Department of Health, Education, and Welfare Final Report, Project No. 1-1-096, 1973.
4. Mathewson, G. "The Effects of Attitude Upon Comprehension of Dialect Folktales," doctoral dissertation, University of California at Berkeley, 1973.
5. Mathewson, G. "Children's Response to Reading and Hearing Standard English and Nonstandard Dialect Stories: A Study of Evaluation and Comprehension," paper presented to the American Education Research Association, New Orleans, 1973.
6. Piestrup, A. "Black Dialect Interference and Accommodation of Reading in First Grade," *Monographs of the Language Behavior Research Laboratory.* Berkeley, California: University of California, 1973.
7. Ruddell, R. "An Investigation of the Effect of the Similarity of Oral and Written Patterns of Language Structure in Reading Comprehension," doctoral dissertation, Indiana University, 1963.

8. Rystrom, R. "Dialect Training and Reading: A Further Look," *Reading Research Quarterly,* 5 (Summer 1970), 581-599.

9. Schaaf, E. "A Study of Black English Syntax and Reading Comprehension," master's seminar study, University of California at Berkeley, 1971.

10. Sims, R. "A Psycholinguistic Description of Miscues Created by Selected Young Readers During Oral Reading of Texts in Black Dialect and Standard English," doctoral dissertation, Wayne State University, 1972.

11. Stewart, W. "On the Use of Negro Dialect in the Teaching of Reading," in J. Baratz and R. Shuy (Eds.), *Teaching Black Children to Read.* Washington, D.C.: Center for Applied Linguistics, 1969, 156-219.

12. Tatham, S. "Reading Comprehension of Materials Written with Select Oral Language Patterns: A Study at Grades Two and Four," *Reading Research Quarterly,* 5 (Spring 1970), 402-426.

13. Venezky, R. "Nonstandard Language and Reading," *Elementary English,* 47 (March 1970), 334-345.

RELEVANT CONTENT FOR
THE BLACK ELEMENTARY SCHOOL PUPIL

Marian L. Vick □ North Carolina A&T State University

Enlightened educators recognize that our educational system has failed in a most fundamental way to provide relevant reading instructional materials for black children. Some may argue that the basic cause of this failure is racism which dictates the choice of reading instructional materials and the way they are presented. Few understand, however, the basic educational issues that revolve around the differences in what is important and critical for black children and what is important for various other ethnic groups.

Those who have grown up as the progeny of black ancestors have generally been provided with a set of experiences that are different from those of the vast majority of Americans. It is these experiences that determine which events are perceived as relevant, irrelevant, or critical. Since many black children have a different reality from their white counterparts, it is important to understand that their priorities may refer to a different ordering system with different needs for the future. Therefore, in order to consider relevant content for the black elementary school pupil in this technological age, the topic must be viewed from the black perspective.

Miller (*12*:130) raises some questions concerning materials for multiethnic learners which may help us to decide what is meant by relevant content for the black elementary pupil.

> Considering the negative results of racism and prejudice and the conflict that exists in the lives of learners who come from minority groups, what change of emphasis in securing curriculum materials is advisable to meet the current situation? Moreover, recognizing the demands that diverse ethnic groups in America make upon their members and the imperative need for some sort of national unity of a democratic kind, what is a relevant education?

To paraphrase the second question, what do we mean by relevant content for the black elementary pupil? In education, the term *relevance*

> ... implies that what is to be learned is perceived by the learner as having meaning in his present life and the expectation that it will have utility in future learning or coping situations. A meaningful relevant education, therefore, includes the skills necessary for one to cope with life. Moreover, this kind of education focuses on content that deals with specific ethnic group experiences in contemporary society and, therefore, with the problems of everyday existence.

Boyer (2:191) defines instructional reading materials as "... those visual and/or audio items which are incorporated into the interactive phase of the instructional act to increase clarity and to enhance achievement."

These definitions provide a basis for selecting relevant content that will help the black elementary school pupil cope with life the way it really is. Black children need to know about their past and they need to learn basic skills, but they should also know very early in their education what they are going to have to face in everyday living.

Until recently, many instructional reading materials were negative in their effect on black pupils because black people were excluded from textbooks, instructional films, filmstrips, educational television, and other supplementary materials. And too, materials and illustrations alluding to blacks were usually degrading and derogatory.

Major Directions and Influences on Relevant Materials

Currently, those who select so-called relevant materials for black children have moved in two major directions. One of these directions is toward eliminating, from existing literature, materials which are degrading or derogatory to a particular ethnic group. The other direction is toward an effort to introduce black children and black themes into the literature for young people.

Although the quest for relevant content for the black child is not exactly a new development, the need is beginning to be recognized. Increased demands for relevance on the part of various ethnic groups, coupled with a social revolution in a technological society, have brought about some accelerating changes. One of the most significant developments in education for black Americans has been the demand on the part of blacks themselves for more relevant curriculum materials.

There are numerous factors which precipitated the demand for more realistic and relevant instructional reading materials for black learners.

A 1965 article by Larrick (*11*) pointing out how few books for black and other minority group children had been published and the House of Representatives hearings in 1966 (*19*) were two major efforts of a strong upsurge of interest in the treatment of racial minorities in books for young children. There were several other reasons for this heightened interest. One was the Elementary and Secondary Education Act of 1965. "Since the act was passed late in the 1964-65 school year, the first money dispensed under it arrived at many schools too late to be used for salaries of new faculty. Therefore, in many instances it was used to purchase textbooks and library books. When schools having many minority group students tried to purchase interracial books with their new money, however, they discovered that much less interracial material existed than what they had hoped to find" (*4*:11).

In addition to the previously mentioned events, ". . . several other studies pointed out that at a very early age, black children learn to feel inferior to white children and white children superior to black children in part because of attitudes communicated to them in the books they read" (*4*:109).

One resulting effect of these forces which demanded more relevant content for black pupils was a reexamination of what, racially speaking, was wrong with children's books. Another resulting effect was the improvement in themes, types of stories, and illustrations in children's books. Black authors and illustrators began to receive more attention. They sometimes became consultants and editors, and interracial children's books appeared more frequently concerned with real life situations of black children.

Interracial basal series like the *Bank Street Readers,* the *Chandler Reading Program, City Schools Reading Program,* and *The World Children Live In* have appeared. And books like *Stevie, Uptown,* and *Train Ride* by John Steptoe, "a gifted black teenage author-artist" (*1*:4), were published by a reputable company. Professional associations like International Reading Association, Children's Librarians, and the National Council of Teachers of English currently devote sessions of their convention programs to the black experience in children's books.

Current Emphases. Efforts to publish and use multiethnic instructional materials for children have met with criticism. In the mid-sixties, newly designed multiracial basal reader series were developed to present a more realistic view of the diversity of American life. Since many beginning readers often are exposed to numerous illustrations in the picture book stories and basal readers, some educators have begun to examine the illustrations and to study their importance in the readers. Parker and Campbell (*15*) conducted a study to examine the illustrations in the *Bank Street Readers, The Language-Experience Readers, The Follett Beginning-To-Read Series,* and the *Reading for Meaning Series.* They also analyzed the relative importance of the illustrations.

In an effort to determine the relative importance of the illustrations, two dimensions were analyzed: the amount of space devoted to pictorial representations and the amount of space devoted to text. They concluded that the new multiracial reader series presented differing pictorial impressions of life associated with a racially mixed world. Though there are some similarities (a large representation of children, emphasis on illustrations to convey meaning, and a good deal of space devoted to illustrations), there are clear differences in the lifestyles pictured in each series and in the nature of the racial representations.

It has been the custom to give careful attention to vocabulary control, word frequency, sentence length, and many other elements in preparing texts for beginning reading. The findings of the Parker and Campbell study, however, indicated that it may be possible to develop criteria to guide illustrators as well, which will help to narrow the gap between the reality of the child's world and the world he sees pictured in books.

Chall (*3*) has pointed out that first grade teachers (if they follow the manuals of basal readers) ask children to devote as much time to "reading" pictures and to discussing their personal experiences as to reading words. Since the attention of children is drawn to illustrations, it appears that more detailed studies of the racial and environmental dimensions might indicate what kinds of impressions racially-mixed world children form as they "read" pictures.

Harris (*7*:126), in commenting on basal readers, has noted, "There are three main trends in regard to content. The first has been a change with regard to characters and their environments. The animals and folk and fairy tales remain, but there has been a recent rather general effort to replace the middle-class white stereotype with ethnic and environmental pluralism. One finds more emphasis on urban settings, on members of minority groups, and on problems related to limited income."

A study by Rose, Zimet, and Blom (*17*:18) concluded that "First graders have demonstrated and identified preferred content in primary reading textbooks in response to single pairs of stories of five content factors. The pranks theme, peer interaction, and same sex activity clearly belong in first grade reading textbooks in greater quantity than they now occur. These content variables do affect the first grader's interest in reading material read to him."

Windley (*20*) comments that recent emphasis upon growth

characteristics, needs, and interests of children at various developmental stages serves to highlight the importance of books which fulfill and satisfy universal needs and interests of *children.* Several universal needs and interests of language and/or instructional materials for young children are identified. "Young children, ages four to seven, are egocentric" (*20*:14). Beyond the self stage, they need materials about persons of their immediate environment, their parents and siblings. Following the egocentric stage comes one of exploration of their everyday world. The need for humor and fantasy is present at any stage of development. There is the need for instructional materials which help the child understand and identify himself. Traditional literature — folk and fairy tales, myths, legends, ballads, folk songs, proverbs, epics, fables — satisfies the need of all children to learn and know about peoples of other lands. Finally, there is the need for realistic instructional materials to provide children an opportunity to explore human problems that are common to all children.

In addition to interracial illustrations in beginning-to-read books and materials which contain universal needs and interests of children, there are growing numbers of good stories, delightfully funny and realistic, where children are children — all colors, sizes, and shapes! Fictional characters are portrayed as doing normal things, common to all children. They can see themselves playing and living near children of every type of religious, national, or racial origin — whether they are living in the city or country, East, West, North, or South. All types of nonfiction are beginning to show blacks in illustrations participating in all facets of American life — social, economic, and geographic. Great strides have been made in science books. Even for the youngest children, we now have a candid discussion of skin color and hair texture. The achievements made by blacks in popular sports have been spectacular. Many fiction and nonfiction books in which blacks appear help to support the idea that one's ability matters far more than his color. In addition, black children are included in all types of readers, picture books, science texts, beginning-to-read stories, and historical material — just as they are represented in most of our major cities, schools, and rural areas.

As Rollins (*16*:xii) notes,

> It has become evident that reading good books can increase the social sensitivity of a child and help him to extend his experiences to gain new insights, appreciations, and understanding of himself and others. Progress has been made . . . ; however, more stories for younger children are needed because it is at this age that a child is introduced to the printed word and the illustrated book. These should build a firm foundation of acceptance so that the child can come to recognize that people are people in spite of their physical differences.

Criteria for Selecting Relevant Content

Some factors to consider in selecting books and other instructional materials for black children are standards of language, appropriate illustrations, universal needs and interests of language for all children, themes, treatment of characters, and realistic human experiences (*1, 6, 8, 10, 12, 13, 18, 20*).

Palmer (*14*:53) states,

> In assessing instructional materials, selection committees must consider a variety of criteria, including how well the materials reflect the multiethnic nature of our society.
>
> Does your school system provide materials that recognize that Americans take pride in their race, religion, and social backgrounds? Does it screen out materials that betray prejudice, perpetuate stereotypes, or fail to recognize the talents, contributions, or aspirations of any segment of the American people?

We must provide the black child with instructional materials which provide real life situations, meaningful experiences, and values that will give him a positive self-image. "In the case of the black child, the need for suitable means to aid him in his search for identity is especially critical. Equally important is the need to provide white children with opportunities to encounter the black experience in honest, human terms" (*18*:20).

Content with universal literary characteristics which appeal to children is as relevant to black children as to any other ethnic group. What black children and adults object to is content filled with stereotyped characterizations, degrading epithets and illustrations, derogatory themes, and artificial obscene language which portray blacks (all inclusive) as objects of derision and ridicule.

In an effort to identify relevant content for the black child, Grant (*6*:11) outlines some major points of the socialization process of a black child. She says,

> The self-image of the black child is formulated during his early socialization process. The self-image results from social interaction and language, with language being the chief means through which an individual learns about his world. Through identification the child takes on the values of others.
>
> . . . The black child must be allowed to identify with those things that provide a positive self-image. His strengths can and ought to be cultivated.

Griffith (*5*:396) says, "America needs the black experience in children's books to achieve a better self-image and to adopt positive role models. White children need the black experience to develop open attitudes towards Blacks. Adults need it to diminish their negative attitudes towards Blacks."

Black children tend to demand reading instructional materials that relate to *now*. Through reading about current problems and difficulties of book characters, children can identify and gain insight into their own problems — problems that arise from loneliness; racial, cultural, or religious differences; growing up; peer relationships; poverty; or physical handicaps (*20*).

The youth of today are concerned with what is going to happen to them in the near future and to the world in the distant future. The task of selecting relevant instructional materials that will help the black elementary school pupil, or any pupil for that matter, to develop into a perceptive, intelligent adult for the future is indeed a difficult and massive task. To aid children in reaching such a goal, Janeczko (*9*) identifies three major areas to be considered in "selecting books for the future-oriented now generation."

The first area to be considered is the environment. The youth of today should be made aware of the environmental crisis in which we are involved and from which we may not be able to extricate ourselves. Content dealing with the care of and reverence for plants, animals, and all the precious things of nature appears relevant for the present generation and those of the future.

Another area of concern is instructional materials that deal with the development of the individual. The black elementary pupil wants to read content that he can understand and with which he can identify. In short, pupils need content about someone who experiences some of the same problems and crises that they are themselves experiencing (*9*).

Finally, materials must be functional. According to Miller (*12*:131) relevant curriculum materials used by teachers ought to serve three related functions: 1) develop basic skills, 2) reflect the ethnicity of the learner, and 3) develop an appreciation for the humanities (art, drama, and music).

To summarize relevant content for the black elementary school pupil, Boyer's words seem appropriately chosen and proper:

> The selection of materials is a *massive* process only because of the growing availability of audio and visual materials on black people in every phase of American life. It is a *significant* process because the use must suggest, in a variety of unique ways, that black students are interested, honest, and capable learners. The most appropriate materials are those which continue to *build the learner's self-concept* and, at the same time, allow him some freedom of self-expression in the utilization process. Because school is generally thought to be an expression of society at large, curricular materials for black learners must also share some resemblance to society.
>
> The most relevant materials are those which communicate in their content that (a) black people are respectable, contributing citizens in

varied endeavors; and (b) black people are *real human beings* capable of love, hate, fear, disappointment, anger, success, and achievement whether they are pictured in the ghetto, in the classroom, in suburbia, or in the rural corners of America.

Perhaps the most damaging curricular materials are those which, by their content, continue to dehumanize black Americans in politics, education, the creative arts, economics, and business. Selectors of curricular materials for black learners must learn and incorporate the "heroes" of the learners into the instructional planning. The production of curricular materials must seek higher levels of authenticity and must reflect all classes and sub-classes of black people — not just the "glamourously poor" alternated with internationally-known issues and famous personalities (*2*:192).

In Conclusion

Not all efforts toward this end have been good. Yet, new emphases, such as interracial textbooks, realistic illustrations, realistic themes and the treatment of characters, the use of language which includes authentic regional vernacular rather than an author-created dialect, and the depiction of blacks in all aspects of human society, represent recent advancements toward the improvement of instructional materials for *all* children. We live in a pluralistic society. Therefore, no one ethnic group or set of experiences should dominate the instructional content to which all children are exposed in our public schools.

Finally, *all* black children are not equally helped with the use of the same kinds of materials. Black children differ among themselves as children of other ethnic groups differ.

Black children have the same basic needs as other youth. Relevant content for them must be accompanied by a sincere belief in their dignity and worth as individuals and learners and by instructional behavior which communicates this belief in the learner's interactive environment.

REFERENCES

1. Baker, Augusta. *The Black Experience in Children's Books.* New York: Public Library, 1971.
2. Boyer, James B. "Materials for Black Learners," *Educational Leadership,* 28 (November 1970), 191-192.
3. Chall, Jeanne. *Learning to Read: The Great Debate.* New York: McGraw-Hill Book Company, 1967.
4. Cornelius, Paul. "Interracial Children's Books: Problems and Progress," *Library Quarterly,* 41 (April 1971), 106-127.
5. Granstrom, Jane, and Anita Silvey. "A Call for Help: Exploring the Black Experience in Children's Books," *Horn Book,* 48 (August 1972), 9-13.

6. Grant, Gwendolyn Goldsley, "The Black Child's Needs," in Harold Tanyzer and Jean Karl (Eds.), *Reading, Children's Books, and Our Pluralistic Society*. Newark, Delaware: International Reading Association, 1972, 9-13.

7. Harris, Albert J. "New Dimensions in Basal Readers," in Howard A. Klein (Ed.), *The Quest for Competency in Teaching Reading*. Newark, Delaware: International Reading Association, 1972, 124-130.

8. Huus, Helen. "Children's Reactions to Books," in Howard A. Klein (Ed.), *The Quest for Competency in Teaching Reading*. Newark, Delaware: International Reading Association, 1972, 25-35.

9. Janeczko, Paul B. "Selecting Books for the Future-Oriented Now Generation," in M. Jerry Weiss, Joseph Brunner, and Warren Heiss (Eds.), *New Perspectives on Paperbacks*. Monograph No. 1. York, Pennsylvania: Strine Printing, 1973, 31-37.

10. Karl, Jean. "Contemporary Children's Literature," in Helen Painter (Ed.), *Reaching Children and Young People Through Literature*. Newark, Delaware: International Reading Association, 1971, 1-18.

11. Larrick, Nancy. "The All-White World of Children's Books," *Saturday Review*, 48 (September 1965), 63-64, 83-85.

12. Miller, Lamar P. "Materials for Multi-Ethnic Learners," *Educational Leadership*, 28 (November 1970), 129-132.

13. NAACP Education Department. *Integrated School Books*. New York: NAACP Education Department, 1967.

14. Palmer, E. B. "Selecting Instructional Materials," *Today's Education*, 61 (February 1972), 53.

15. Parker, Lenore D., and Ellen E. Campbell. "A Look at Illustrations in Multi-Racial First Grade Readers," *Elementary English*, 48 (January 1971), 67-74.

16. Rollins, Charlemae. *We Build Together*. Champaign, Illinois: National Council of Teachers of English, 1967.

17. Rose, Cynthia, Sara Zimet, and Gaston Blom. "Content Counts: Children Have Preferences in Reading Textbook Stories," *Elementary English*, 49 (January 1972), 14-19.

18. Strickland, Dorothy. "The Black Experience in Paperback," in M. Jerry Weiss, Joseph Brunner, and Warren Heiss (Eds.), *New Perspectives on Paperbacks*. Monograph No. 1. York, Pennsylvania: Strine Printing, 1973, 20-23.

19. U.S. Congress, House, Ad Hoc Subcommittee on De Facto School Segregation, Committee on Education and Labor. *Books for Schools and the Treatment of Minorities*, 89th Congress, 1966.

20. Windley, Vivian O. "Literature – A Universal Language," in Howard A. Klein (Ed.), *The Quest for Competency in Teaching Reading*. Newark, Delaware: International Reading Association, 1972, 11-20.

BILINGUALISM, THE SCHOOL, AND THE CHICANO: A POINT OF VIEW

David Conde □ Southern Colorado State College

Educators have traditionally responded negatively to bilingualism because they feel that the presence of more than one language "clutters up" the mind of the learner and interferes with the learning process in the classroom (5). Several intelligence tests designed to contrast the ability of monolingual and bilingual students have indicated that an association can be made between bilinguals and low intelligence ratings (3, 4, 8).

The evidence which associates bilingualism with low IQ scores has subsequently been judged inaccurate. Diebold (5) points out that tests of this type must include groups which are comparable in key extralinguistic dimensions. The tests which link low intelligence ratings to the bilingual were to have contrasted matched monolingual and bilingual groups. The groups turned out not to be comparable in several important areas. For example, the monolinguals involved came from the sociolinguistic dominant group while most of the bilinguals did not. Also, in most cases, the bilinguals were socio-economically disadvantaged; in other words, the groups were not comparable. In addition, the tests themselves used English as the language medium which automatically favored the dominant group.

New developments and procedures have resulted in more realistic and valid information relative to bilingualism. For example, Peal and Lambert after a careful contrastive comparison involving the bilingual French-English Canadian in Montreal, determined that bilingualism has the capability of facilitating a superior performance on both verbal and nonverbal intelligence tests. It was revealed that the wider experiences in two cultures have given the bilingual child "a mental flexibility, a superiority in concept formation; and a more diversified set of mental abilities, in the sense that the patterns of abilities developed by bilinguals were more heterogeneous" (9:20).

These developments suggest a potential richness in the personality make-up of the bilingual, as the degree of ability to form concepts can determine the rate of intellectual growth of the individual.

The School and the Bilingual Chicano

The school, for the most part, has evidenced very little response to the need for exploiting the potential represented by bilingualism. Instead, it continues to treat bilingualism as a disadvantege to be corrected. This is not surprising as the institutional structure and orientation does not allow the school to adequately serve the needs of the bilingual community. Educators, especially in the Southwest, are becoming increasingly concerned and vocal about the institutional thrust in this area (1).

Cardenas (2) points out that one of the principle reasons why the school has been unable to serve the needs of the Chicano child is that its present orientation defines the bilingual student who comes into the classroom as an atypical learner. Educational programs operating in the school are designed for the Anglo-Saxon, English-speaking, middle-class population. As such, they produce a certain amount of compatibility with the typical learner from the majority group. However, if the child is not English-speaking or white or is disadvantaged, incompatibilities between the characteristics of the learner and the instructional program develop. According to Cardenas (2:11).

> ... it is these incompatibilities that exist that lead to, first, the problem performance of children, Mexican-American and black children, and disadvantaged children in our American schools, but in addition to this, I think that unless the incompatibilities are eliminated, that we will not be able to ever achieve better performance on the part of the children.

Many educators have recognized these incompatibilities, and experimental efforts to resolve the differences between the Chicano bilingual and the monolingual institution have been stimulated by federal funds made available for the disadvantaged learner. Many of the programs are compensatory in nature as they are designed to correct difficiencies in children who do not conform to the expectations of the educational institution. The programs for the most part, however, lack both the proper direction and the necessary institutional commitment to resolve the problems.

Compensatory Programs

Compensatory programs, by their very definition, sanction approaches designed to act upon the atypical learner in order to make him compatible with the thrust of the institutional programs.

The tragic thing about this emphasis is that the burden for change is placed squarely on the shoulders of the child rather than on the school. From the first time the Mexican-American enters the classroom, he is asked to pursue goals which may cause him to reject his background and the cultural "baggage" he brings from his home, thus shattering the wholeness of identity necessary for healthy self-actualization.

Institutional Commitment

Compensatory programs in the school are, more often than not, federally funded and as such do not have the permanency of the normal programs which are locally funded. This appears to be one of the major reasons for the relative lack of commitment institutions seem to have to these programs. For example, many of the programs are run as appendages to the permanent structure and can be easily removed when federal funds are no longer forthcoming.

The lack of commitment on the part of local institutions has brought many complaints from federal administrators who seek to effect genuine influence for positive change. Despite some success, the overall track record of compensatory programs is disappointing. Illich (6:3) notes that between 1965 and 1968 over three billion dollars were spent in the schools throughout the nation without bringing significant improvement. This lack of adequate progress has in turn become a source of deep frustration for those communities supporting the schools, and no amount of rationalization can erase their misgivings (7).

A Mandate for Change

A mandate for effective change is clear. This change should feature a development toward making the school more responsible to its community constituency. As Cardenas (2:12), states:

> There is no way that you can make an Anglo-Saxon out of a Mexican-American, and efforts to eliminate a dominant language have been unsuccessful, and it is fairly obvious that if we are going to enjoy immediate success it is necessary that we abandon these efforts to change the characteristics of the child and do something about changing the characteristics of the institutional programs, so that it will be compatible with the characteristics of the child.

In reflecting the characteristics of the Chicano child, the school should also reflect the culturally based environment of the bilingual community it serves. A thrust such as this can best serve the needs of our pluralistic society.

Program Model

Programs must be instituted which have a positive influence on the childhood voyage toward self-actualization. They should be geared to 1) change the perspective of the Chicano from a pathological to a positive force which can create a healthy self-concept, 2) reduce the trauma of separation of the child from the home as he enters and undergoes the formal educational process, and 3) build on the linguistic and other cultural baggage the child brings from home.

The programs should take into consideration the sociocultural characteristics of the student and his community. Bilingual models such as those Valencia (*11*) reviews and outlines can provide direction relative to the medium of instruction. However, the starting point of the formal education experience for the bilingual Chicano must be those structures and orientation he has already acquired before entering the school. By this is meant that if English is the subject, it may have to be taught as a foreign language. Other children may have to be taught in English or Spanish or both until the stronger language in terms of overall use is developed for complete articulation. This is not to say that English should not become the medium of instruction at some point; however, it does not have to possess the priority that it presently has since the immediate needs for instructional delivery (in terms of language) can be satisfied by other languages, such as Spanish. At the same time, the delivery of subject matter instruction should be filtered through the cultural perspective which will strengthen the child's psyche whenever possible. The rich heritage of the Mexican-American can provide the resource for actualizing a positive identity on the part of the Chicano child.

It is therefore necessary to redirect the efforts of the school toward reflecting compatibility with the community it serves. At the same time, schools can eliminate the bankrupt image of compensatory programs designed to assist the Mexican-American by channeling their work into the area of facilitating institutional change. Under these new conditions those things the Chicano child brings to the school in terms of cognitive development and cultural orientation will become the starting point for the formal educational experience rather than a disadvantage to be corrected. Bilingualism will no longer be a problem to be resolved; rather, it will be an asset to be exploited and rewarded.

REFERENCES

1. Arciniega, Tomas. "The Myth of Compensatory Education," unpublished manuscript, 1972.

2. Cardenas, Jose. Testimony to the United States District Court in Tyler, Texas, July 1971.

3. Darcy, N. T. "A Review of the Literature on the Effects of Bilingualism upon the Measurements of Intelligence," *Journal of Genetic Psychology*, 82 (1953), 21-57.

4. Darcy, N. T. "Bilingualism and the Measurement of Intelligence: Review of a Decade of Research," *Journal of Genetic Psychology*, 103 (1963), 259-282.

5. Diebold, A. Richard, Jr. "The Consequences of Early Bilingualism in Cognitive Development and Personality Formation," Educational Resources Information Center, 1966. (ED 020 491)

6. Illich, Ivan. *Deschooling Society*. New York: Harper and Row, 1971.

7. Jablonsky, Adelaide. "Status Report on Compensatory Education," Information Retrieval Center on the Disadvantaged, Horace Mann-Lincoln Institute, Teachers College, Columbia University, 7 (Winter-Spring 1971).

8. Jensen, J. V. "Effects of Early Bilingualism," *Elementary English*, 39 (1962), 132-143, 358-366.

9. Peal, E., and Lambert, W. E. "The Relation of Bilingualism to Intelligence," *Psychological Monographs*, No. 546 (1962).

10. Valencia, Atilano. *Bilingual-Bicultural Education for the Spanish-English Bilingual*. Las Vegas, New Mexico: New Mexico Highlands University Press, 1972.

SOURCES FOR FURTHER LEARNING: SECTION 1

☐ Baxter, K. "Combating the Influence of Black Stereotypes in Children's Books," *Reading Teacher,* 27 (March 1974), 540-544.

☐ Brunner, J. "Reading and Urban Education: An Analysis of Some Traditional and Emerging Premises," in T. Barrett and D. Johnson (Eds.), *Views on Elementary Reading Instruction.* Newark, Delaware: International Reading Association, 1973, 31-39.

☐ Bryant, W. "Counteracting the Problem of Negative Stereotyping," in T. Barrett and D. Johnson (Eds.), *Views on Elementary Reading Instruction.* Newark, Delaware: International Reading Association, 1973, 22-30.

☐ Burling, R. *English in Black and White.* New York: Holt, 1973.

☐ Garcia, R. "Mexican-American Bilingualism and English Language Development," *Journal of Reading,* 17 (March 1974), 467-473.

☐ Goodman, K., and C. Buck. "Dialect Barriers to Reading Comprehension Revisited," *Reading Teacher,* 27 (October 1973), 6-12.

☐ Hodges, R., and E. Rudorf (Eds.). *Language and Learning to Read: What Teachers Should Know About Language.* Boston: Houghton Mifflin, 1972.

☐ Johns, J. "What Do Innercity Children Prefer to Read?" *Reading Teacher,* 26 (February 1973), 462-467.

☐ Justin, N. "Mexican-American Reading Habits and Their Cultural Basis," *Journal of Reading,* 16 (March 1973), 467-473.

☐ Koss, H. "Relevancy and Children's Literature," *Elementary English,* 49 (November 1972), 991-992.

☐ Laffey, J., and R. Shuy (Eds.). *Language Differences: Do They Interfere?* Newark, Delaware: International Reading Association, 1973.

☐ Mattila, R. "As I See Spanish-Speaking Students," *Reading Teacher,* 26 (March 1973), 605-608.

☐ Shuy, R. "Teacher Training and Urban Language Problems," in R. Fasold and R. Shuy (Eds.), *Teaching Standard English in the Inner City.* Washington, D.C.: Center for Applied Linguistics, 1970, 120-141.

☐ Smith, H. "Standard or Nonstandard: Is There an Answer?" *Elementary English,* 50 (February 1973), 225-233, 241.

☐ Wheat, T. "Reading and the Culturally Diverse," *Elementary English,* 51 (February 1974), 251-256, 261.

INTELLIGENCE, SEX, AND READING ACHIEVEMENT

FOCUS QUESTIONS

- Are schools responsible for helping students become literate?
- Is there always a relationship between IQ and achievement?
- Are there differences in learning and retention abilities among students with different IQs?
- What qualities characterize successful ghetto schools?
- Are girls better readers than boys?
- What educational practices might help alleviate sex differences in learning to read?

RELATIONSHIPS AMONG IQ, LEARNING ABILITY, AND READING ACHIEVEMENT

S. Jay Samuels □ University of Minnesota
and
Patricia R. Dahl □ Bloomington, Minnesota, Schools

This paper is concerned with the accountability and responsibility of schools in helping students achieve levels of literacy sufficient for them to comprehend the reading materials with which they will be confronted (2). Pertinent topics such as the role of IQ in reading achievement, the relationship between IQ and learning ability, and characteristics of ghetto schools where reading is taught successfully will be presented.

Responsibility for Success and Failure in Learning

When teachers are asked to explain why some students are underachievers, we are frequently told the students may be immature, have specific learning disabilities, or lack innerdrive. Conversely, when teachers are asked why some students are overachievers, we are frequently told the teaching method is effective. It is interesting to note that student failure is explained by internal factors over which the teacher has little control, whereas success is explained by external factors over which the teacher has significant control. Thus, teachers tend to take credit for success, while placing responsibility for failure on the student (1).

The position taken in this paper is that nearly all children, including the educable retarded, can be literate. Goldiamond and Dyrud (7) expressed this position quite well when they wrote: "The performance of the student may be to a considerable extent a function of the procedures used to establish that behavior; we should look to deficits in our own procedures before ascribing deficits to the students or difficulty to the problem."

IQ and Achievement

In Jensen's famous article on IQ and achievement (9), the contributions of heredity and environment to IQ and achievement are discussed. According to Jensen, most of the differences in IQ can be accounted for by genetic factors, over which the school has no control. On the other hand, most of the differences in achievement can be accounted for by environmental factors, over which the school has considerable control, at least in terms of school environment. Most educators would agree that it is achievement, not IQ, for which the school is primarily responsible. It is fortunate, indeed, that in the area over which the school has responsibility it also has a measure of control.

Most educators know there is a substantial relationship between IQ and reading achievement. Correlations are generally in the neighborhood of .50 to .60. What must be kept in mind is that correlation does not imply causation. Because two variables, such as IQ and reading, are related, it does not necessarily mean that one is cause and the other is effect. If IQ were a powerful determinant of reading success, it would be difficult to explain what many have observed, namely that some low IQ children outperform children with much higher IQs.

IQ and Learning Ability

Rohwer and others (*13*) claim "intelligence tests rarely require the child to engage in learning; they require him to give evidence that he has learned something previously." Consequently, it is important to overcome the tendency to think of IQ as a measure of learning ability.

Rohwer is critical of the IQ as a measure of learning efficiency because it is premised upon the false assumption that all children of a given chronological age have had equal opportunity to learn what is asked on the tests. When an IQ test asks the child to point to a picture of a plate with a "chip" on it, or asks him to find the picture of a "silhouette," it assumes that the children taking the test have had equal exposure to these concepts.

Obviously, children from certain home backgrounds will have had greater exposure to the concepts used in the tests. It is also probable that the same home conditions which foster vocabulary building will also encourage high achievement. Dave (*3*), for example, found that identification of home conditions such as parental aspirations for the child, achievement praise, intellectuality in the home work habits, academic guidance, and parental language models were better predictors of reading achievement than were IQ or socioeconomic status. While it is true that the IQ is a good predictor of academic achievement, it is increasingly falling into disrepute as a measure of basic learning potential.

Reducing the Correlation Between IQ and Achievement

Under certain conditions there is essentially no relationship between IQ and achievement. For example, when a learning task is simple, low and high IQ children score high in achievement. When a learning task is extremely difficult, low and high IQ children score low in achievement. In both cases there is a lack of correlation between IQ and achievement. A correlation between IQ and achievement, however, exists when task difficulty is of an intermediate level and time-to-learn is fixed for all students.

If one wishes to reduce the correlation between IQ and achievement, the task facing the educator entails simplifying the task, ensuring that prerequisite skills are mastered, developing motivational procedures to keep the student on the task, and allocating a sufficient amount of time to the student so that he can master the task.

The importance of simplifying a task was demonstrated by Stolurow (20). He developed an easy and a more difficult program sequence to teach fractions. In the easy program he found achievement differed little between low and high ability groups. With the more difficult program, the high ability group obtained much higher scores than did the low ability groups. In this study one finds that in the easy program the correlation between IQ and achievement was reduced, but in the more difficult program the usual correlation between IQ and achievement was found.

Eigen and Feldhusen (4) gave ninth graders a program on sets, relations, and functions. They found virtually no relationship between IQ and achievement (r= -.07), when pretest and scores on the Iowa Tests of Basic Skills were partialed out. We note, then, when prior achievement is partialed out, there is little of predictive value left in the IQ score. This finding supports Rohwer's contention that IQ tests primarily measure prior learning. Eigen and Feldhusen state that for purposes of grouping, degree of mastery of prerequisite skills is superior to grouping by IQ scores.

The importance of mastering prerequisite skills was demonstrated by Gagne (6). In his study, no student passed the final test who had not mastered the prerequisite skills. When the students were taught the subordinate skills they were able to pass the criterion test. Gagne's position is that if a teaching program is effective, and if the students are given enough time, everyone will master the prerequisite skills and pass the final test. Thus, the correlation between IQ and achievement can be reduced to zero.

At the present time, one of the major obstacles standing in the way of subskill mastery is that many students are not given enough time to learn and master the material before they are introduced to a new task. One reason for this is that in many teaching situations time-to-learn a particular concept is fixed for all students. Those who have mastered the prerequisite skills may master the new concept in the time allocated; however, the students who have not mastered the prerequisite skills often find they cannot master the new skill in the amount of time given to the task. Although some attempt has been made in the classroom to adjust for the individual time needs of students through adjustable grouping procedures and nongraded classes, the teacher may be unaware of particular student needs. In general, we have very poor evaluation systems to monitor the progress of each child. In the absence of good evaluation systems for each student, it is easy to advance a child to a new skill before he is ready.

No Difference in Basic Learning Abilities

Recent research has found virtually no difference in basic learning ability among individuals who differ considerably in IQ. Samuels and Anderson (*15*) gave a simple associational learning task to third graders who differed significantly in IQ. They found no difference between the two IQ groups in learning these associations.

Zeaman and House (*23*) used a discrimination learning task with three groups of retarded learners who differed in IQ. The acquisition curves for the groups indicated a period in which performance was at the chance level. Once the critical dimensions of difference in the stimuli were noticed, there was a rapid rise in percent correct. The lowest IQ group took the longest to note the critical stimulus dimensions and the highest IQ group took the least time to note the critical stimulus features. Comparisons of the three acquisition curves showed no difference; only an attentional variable (the amount of time needed to note the stimulus differences) differentiated the three IQ groups. Estes (*5*:166) concluded that "individuals of differing intelligence develop different habits of attention and stimulus selection. But they do not differ greatly with respect to learning ability in the sense of rate of formation of association or retention of associations once formed." If habits of attention and stimulus selection are important, then controlling the orienting behavior of students and directing their attention to the dimension of difference among stimuli should facilitate learning. Samuels and Turnure (*16*) found that attentiveness (task orienting behavior) was significantly correlated with reading achievement. Samuels (*14*) was able to produce nearly twice the learning rate in an associational learning task by directing the student's attention to the critical dimension of difference aspects of the stimuli.

In other studies of basic learning ability, Kee and Rohwer (*10*), Rohwer, et al. (*13*), Green (*8*), and Semler and Iscoe (*19*) found no difference in actual tests of learning performance among individuals who differed considerably in IQ.

No Difference in Retention

Just as laboratory tests have found no difference in basic learning ability among individuals who differ in IQ, laboratory tests have failed to find differences in retention. Studies over a considerable period of time by Underwood (20), Klausmeier and Feldhusen (12), Shuell and Keppel (18), and Shuell (17) have failed to find differences either in short or long term retention related to IQ, provided level of original learning is controlled.

The laboratory finding of no difference in retention lies in the face of common observations of information retention in the classroom. In the classroom, one finds that high IQ students have superior retention in comparison to lower IQ students. This observation has led many to believe there is a strong relationship between IQ and recall. However, the observation that there is a relationship between IQ and recall is an artifact produced by the fact that in the typical classroom, the time allocated for the acquisition of concepts, skills, and new information is usually fixed. If the teacher sets the pace of instruction to the middle IQ group, then the high IQ group will overlearn, the middle group will master the task, and the low IQ group will probably fail to master the task. Differences in classroom tests of recall under these conditions simply reflect differences in the level of original acquisition of information.

Successful Ghetto Schools

Generally, the lower the socioeconomic status of students, the less well will they do on achievement tests. In the typical inner-city school, reading achievement is far below national norms; however, this need not necessarily be the case. Weber (22) selected four ghetto schools where third grade reading achievement equalled or exceeded national norms and where the schools were on the same level as schools with average income enrollments. By comparing the successful ghetto schools with the less successful ghetto schools, Weber found the following identifiable qualities in the successful schools which were absent in many of the others:

1. *Strong leadership.* Each school had clearly identifiable individuals who were respected by teachers and pupils and who placed great emphasis on reading. These individuals were either principals or superintendents.

2. *High expectations.* A "can do" success oriented philosophy prevaded the school, from principal to students.

3. *Strong emphasis on reading.* Reading received the major priority in the first three grades.

4. *Reading specialists.* Each of the schools had trained reading personnel who helped the teachers. In some cases the reading specialist trained teacher aides to provide actual reading instruction. Thus, the regular classroom teacher was able to divide the class into smaller groups for instruction.

5. *Use of phonics.* Although two of the schools used nonphonic readers, their programs were supplemented with phonics materials.

6. *Evaluation.* Individual student progress was monitored regularly as a way to make appropriate instructional decisions for that child.

All of these factors created a "sense of purpose, relative quiet, and pleasure in learning." Many of the other schools studied were filled with "disorder, noise, tension, and confusion." A conclusion found in the Weber study was that reading failure usually is the fault of the schools, not the children nor their backgrounds.

Although Weber places the entire burden of responsibility on the schools, the authors of this article believe this is unjustified. School personnel are sincere in their effort to help all children achieve satisfactory levels of literacy. The goal of literacy for nearly all of our students is not one which is easily achieved. Furthermore, many of our schools are working under various kinds of handicaps such as lack of highly trained experts in reading and information gaps on optional ways to teach reading, which still remain to be researched. If our public schools are to be held responsible for both success and failure in reading, they should share this responsibility with colleges and universities which train teachers and are better equipped to do the research needed to provide answers to questions on the pedagogy of reading.

For too long there has been a tendency for university researchers and subject matter experts to separate themselves from becoming part of the instructional team in school systems. On the other hand, public school people have seemed willing to engage in their tasks without seeking help from the university. There are several examples of the facilitation of the learning which results when public school and university personnel work together. What is needed, we believe, are close cooperative partnerships between our public schools and our universities for the purpose of bringing literacy to all.

REFERENCES

1. Baldwin, T. L., T. J. Johnson, and D. E. Wiley. "The Teacher's Perception and Attribution of Causation," paper presented at the annual meeting of the American Educational Research Association, Minneapolis, 1970.

2. Bormuth, John R. "Illiteracy in the Suburbs," unpublished manuscript, University of Chicago, 1970.

3. Dave, R. H. "The Identification and Measurement of Environmental Process Variables That Are Related to Educational Achievement," doctoral dissertation, University of Chicago, 1963.

4. Eigen, Lewis D., and John Feldhusen. "Interrelationships Among Attitude, Achievement, Reading, Intelligence, and Transfer Variables in Programmed Instruction," in J. P. De Cecco (Ed.), *Educational Technology.* New York: Holt, 1964, 376-386.

5. Estes, William K. *Learning Theory and Mental Development.* New York: Academic Press, 1970.

6. Gagne, Robert M. "The Acquisition of Knowledge," *Psychological Review,* 69 (1962), 355-365.

7. Goldiamond, I., and J. E. Dyrud. "Reading as Operant Behavior," in J. Money (Ed.), *The Disabled Reader: Education of the Dyslexic Child.* Baltimore, Maryland: Johns Hopkins Press, 1966, 93-115.

8. Green, R. B. "SES Differences on Learning and Ability Tests in Black Children," unpublished master's thesis, University of California at Berkeley, 1969.

9. Jensen, A. R. "How Much Can We Boost IQ and Scholastic Achievement?" *Harvard Educational Review,* 39 (Winter-Summer 1969), 1-123.

10. Kee, Daniel W., and William D. Rohwer, Jr. "Noun-Pair Learning in Four Ethnic Groups: Conditions of Presentation and Response," *Integrated Education,* 10 (November 1972), 29-32.

11. Keppel, G. "Verbal Learning and Memory," *Annual Review of Psychology,* 19 (1968), 169-202.

12. Klausmeier, Herbert J., and John F. Feldhusen. "Retention in Arithmetic Among Children of Low, Average, and High Intelligence at 117 Months of Age," *Journal of Educational Psychology,* 50 (April 1959), 88-92.

13. Rohwer, William D., Jr. et al. "Population Differences and Learning Proficiency," *Journal of Educational Psychology,* 62 (1971), 1-14.

14. Samuels, S. J. "Effect of Distinctive Feature Training on Paired-Associate Learning," *Journal of Educational Psychology,* 64 (April 1973), 164-170.

15. Samuels, S. J., and R. H. Anderson. "Visual Memory, Paired-Associate Learning, and Reading," *Journal of Educational Psychology,* in press.

16. Samuels, S. J., and J. E. Turnure. "Attention and Reading Achievement in First Grade Boys and Girls," *Journal of Educational Psychology,* 66 (February 1974), 29-32.

17. Shuell, Thomas J. *Individual Differences in Learning and Retention.* Final Report, State University of New York at Buffalo, 1972.

18. Shuell, Thomas J., and Geoffrey Keppel. "Learning Ability and Retention," *Journal of Educational Psychology,* 61 (February 1970), 59-65.

19. Semler, I. J., and I. Iscoe. "Comparative and Developmental Study of the Learning Abilities of Negro and White Children Under Four Conditions," *Journal of Educational Psychology,* 54 (February 1963), 38-54.

20. Stolurow, Lawrence M. "Social Impact on Programmed Instruction: Aptitudes and Abilities Revisited," in J. P. De Cecco (Ed.), *Educational Technology*. New York: Holt, 1964, 348-355.

21. Underwood, B., and R. Schulz. *Meaningfulness and Verbal Learnings*. Philadelphia: Lippincott, 1960.

22. Weber, George. "Inner-city Children Can Be Taught to Read: Four Successful Schools," Washington, D.C.: Council for Basic Education, 1971.

23. Zeaman, D., and B. J. House. "The Role of Attention in Retardate Discrimination Learning," in N. R. Ellis (Ed.), *Handbook of Mental Deficiency*. New York: McGraw-Hill, 1963, 159-223.

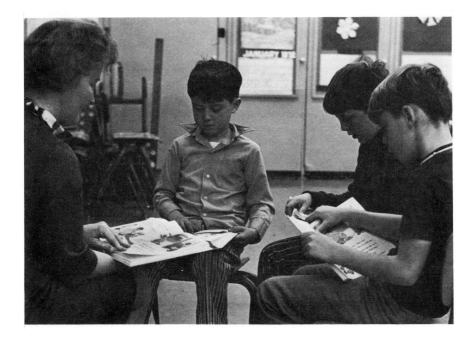

BOYS' RIGHT TO READ: SEX FACTORS IN LEARNING TO READ

Richard Kolczynski □ Ohio State University

Although the amount of research data on the topic of sex differences and learning is voluminous, conclusive statements of significant differences are somewhat less available. Methodology and experimentation often confuse and cloud the results of potentially significant and useful studies. Less technical, but more heated and probably the basis for much of the controversy, is the amount of variation that exists among psychologists, sociologists, and educators as to the origin, development, and significance of sex differences. Numerous studies support the biological as well as the cultural basis of sex differences. While it may be true that most American psychologists have supported the cultural determinants of such differences, newer research and the reexamination of older studies have lead to rather convincing arguments for ultimate biological origins. Such dichotomous arguments may prove fruitless, however, since it hardly seems possible to separate the nature-nurture variables contributing to sex differences. The most reasonable hypothesis, at this point, appears to be one that credits the interactional workings of innumerable biological and cultural forces.

One's point of view as to the origin of sex differences affects how one describes and justifies the various differences found among boys and girls throughout their early years. As one psychologist (12) has claimed, those who side with cultural determinants stress the expectations placed upon boys and girls by our society. In other words, society consists of male and female members with each group having established identities and roles to be followed. The child, according to this theory, learns his role in society through sex-stereotypic upbringing. On the other hand, those supporting a biological foundation tend to see differences as products of constitutional origin.

Society's expectations, therefore, are merely reflective of its experiences with two kinds of children.

Although these arguments are almost unending, an important fact still remains. Boys and girls differ in many ways. Aside from the obvious physiological differences, certain behavioral differences are evident. As early as one year of age, boys are already more active and explorative, while girls are passive and more dependent upon their mothers (4). In addition, parents have already demonstrated differential behavior toward the two sexes.

One particular aspect influenced by factors in the environment, and favoring girls, is language development. Numerous studies (6, 7, 11, 18) have found that girls develop speech earlier than do boys, articulate more clearly, use sentences earlier, use less slang, and have a larger vocabulary. In general, girls develop language competency at a faster rate than boys, especially when IQ and socioeconomic status are held constant. It is also important to note that boys are the victims of speech defects in a significantly greater proportion than girls (6, 7, 10, 20). Two widely accepted hypotheses are offered in explanation of these differences. One is that mothers do not reinforce boys for their speech habits (or imitations) as much as they do with girls (6, 7). Because of greater contact with their mothers, girls imitate their speech habits much more readily than boys. The second hypothesis is that boys, because of their active, explorative nature and their preoccupation with objects, have less need for verbalization, especially in communicative and interpersonal situations (11).

These arguments must be reexamined today since many more mothers work and are away from both boys and girls. Also, newer games, television programs, children's books, and a variety of other activities now give increased attention to boys and induce greater verbal response. Finally, more recent studies (1, 2, 9, 14) dealing with the various complexities of language, rather than speech alone, have not shown significant differences between the sexes.

Sex Differences and Reading

One statement that can hardly be debated is that girls, as a group, show significantly higher achievement in learning to read than boys. Loughlin and his associates (5), in an attempt to discover the relationships between anxiety and achievement among elementary school children, studied the differences between the sexes by intelligence, subject matter, grade, and achievement level. The entire population of grades four through eight in an urban-suburban school district was given a series of tests including the California Reading Test. In general, the results support the hypothesis that girls generally attain higher mean anxiety scores than do boys. Such findings "suggest that sex differences in anxiety manifest themselves early in children's academic careers, reach a peak in the fifth or sixth grade, and diminish considerably by the time the eighth grade is attained."

In a study of over thirteen thousand students in grades two through eight, Gates (3) found the mean raw score for girls higher than that for boys on twenty-one comparisons of the Gates Reading Survey tests. In addition, a "relatively large proportion of boys obtained the lowest scores without a corresponding increase in the number obtaining top scores." The results of the study revealed that boys obtained lower mean scores in reading ability throughout elementary school. Evidence from the U.S.O.E. First Grade Studies also indicates sex differences in reading. It was generally found that mean scores were in favor of girls on readiness measures, first grade achievement tests, and on tests given to the groups that continued the experiments through the second grade. In addition, another large-scale study reported that girls did better than boys on all reading skills at three school ages (13).

Several interesting studies have attempted to find appropriate methods of instruction or grouping that would minimize sexual differences in learning to read. McNeil (8) conducted a study that compared boys and girls who learned to read through two approaches — programed instruction versus direct instruction by female teachers. An auto-instructional program in reading was presented to the children when they were in kindergarten. The children were then tested on word recognition. The same group were later enrolled as first graders and received instruction from female teachers. Again, the students were tested after four months of instruction in addition to being interviewed individually.

The results of programed instruction, as revealed on the criterion test, indicated that the boys obtained significantly higher scores than the girls. The criterion test administered after direct teacher instruction, however, showed that these same boys were inferior to the girls. In addition, analysis of the taped interviews revealed that boys received more negative admonitions than girls and boys were given less opportunity to read. Evidence from McNeil's findings support the hypothesis that boys are treated differently than girls and that such treatment by teachers affects achievement in beginning reading.

Several researchers have attempted to measure differences in reading achievement between boys and girls after instruction was provided in sex-segregated groups. Wyatt (19) focused attention on first graders by recognizing and utilizing sex differences as a criterion for grouping. After a 140-day instructional period, all children were given a series of reading tests. Although no significant differences were evident among boys in different teaching approaches, it was generally found that girls as a group had significantly higher scores when compared with those of all boys. Wyatt concluded that the lag found among boys appeared dependent upon factors other than grouping and teaching approach.

Tagatz (*17*) and Stanchfield (*16*) also studied sex-segregated grouping. While Tagatz found that personal adjustment was significantly increased as a result of sex grouping, test results revealed no significant differences in reading achievement. Stanchfield also found that boys did not learn to read better as a result of such grouping. It appears evident that boys and girls can profit by remaining together for instruction.

One additional finding, a classic in this area, should be mentioned. Preston (*15*) conducted a study in which he compared the reading achievement of German students with that of American students. Fourth and sixth grade students were used in both countries. Each group of students took two reading tests: the Frankfurter Test and the Gates Reading Survey. Both tests were translated so that each pupil took the tests in his native language. When the mean scores were compared, it was found that American girls excelled in reading over American boys. The reverse was true with the German sample. Preston also reported that although the incidence of reading retardation is greater among boys in America, the reverse is found among German students. Preston suggested that one explanation for the pattern found among the German sample was the predominance of male teachers in Germany. He further concluded that the evidence provides reason to believe that sex differences in reading stem from possible cultural or environmental conditions.

Educational Implications

Studies dealing with sex differences in learning to read provide information concerning the incidence of such phenomena. They also cite possible causal factors and recommend practices to help alleviate or reduce the differences. The following suggestions and implications are offered to administrators as well as classroom teachers. Although these suggestions and recommendations are presented from the personal point of view of this writer (influenced by *his* sex), they can be supported by studies in psychology, teaching methodology, and/or simple common sense.

Language. Most educators are at least minimally familiar with the vast amount of research giving evidence of the slower language development of boys. The fact that many differences in language development are culturally determined is also understood by a large number of teachers. Would it not be logical, therefore, to assume that basic language instruction (including reading) would not be exactly the same for boys as for girls at a given time in most situations? In accepting this assumption, one immediately questions the apparent gap and loss between factual knowledge and classroom practice. Knowledge of such differences is valuable only to the extent that adjustments are made in aspects of the school program effecting the growth and development of language skills. The reading readiness period is a particularly important phase of reading that demands attention to the language facility of each child. It is essential that the linguistically immature child does not become frustrated with reading at any time because of inadequate attention to his language needs.

Behavior and interests. One hardly needs years of teaching experience to note the general behavior pattern of boys. Most boys tend to engage in activities that are physically active and require minimal amounts of verbal interaction. Furthermore, such play usually takes place in areas away from adult language models. In addition to certain natural tendencies toward "boy type" activity, our society exerts a considerable amount of pressure upon boys to develop the stereotyped male image. Suffice it to say that reading ability does not appear on any list of criteria measuring one's masculinity.

Within the realm of reading instruction, boys again have interests apart from the female-oriented content of some reading texts. Most boys tend to delight in the active, fast-moving adventures of "real" (in the sense of quality of characterization) animals and people as opposed to the sterility found in many children's books. In addition to appropriate library books, many other materials such as comic books and sports magazines may spark an interest in reading, and interest, in turn, sparks learning. An efficient teacher is one who provides a wide variety of books and materials to meet the interests and needs of students.

Feminine schools. The typical elementary school supports and often demands many traits and qualities that are characteristic of female domination: quiet, nonaggressive behavior; conformity to rules, regulations, curriculum, and teacher styles; neatness, cleanliness, manners, and posture; emphasis upon verbal interaction and passive activities. It is important for teachers to be able to recognize when these forces of female domination are adversely affecting the learning atmosphere for boys. A teacher who provides opportunities for development and personal expression will find her pupils more easily motivated to participate in a wide variety of activities. Over-insistence upon conformity toward behavior patterns that are characteristically feminine could only result in frustration and alienation that may affect boys' lifetime learning (reading) habits.

Needless to say, the emergence of more male teachers would help counterbalance some of the difficulties of the feminine school. It is important, however, that the male teacher not become totally engulfed and transformed by the existing system. Mere physical sex is not as significant as the identity and role exhibited by the male teacher. It is crucial that one regards all persons as having traits that will fall on a continuum of feminine and masculine characteristics. One's placement on such a continuum would probably prove more significant than mere labeling as male/female according to sex. Furthermore, a balance between male and female personnel would be more appropriate and democratic than domination by either sex.

Incentive. Perhaps one of the most important aspects of the teaching and learning process is the motivational stimulation provided for each activity. In addition to this external stimulation, some activities contain a certain amount of incentive within themselves. Unfortunately, the act of reading is usually found to contain less incentive for boys than for girls. Elementary school boys usually have fewer motives and less need for reading than do girls. Consequently, it becomes of paramount importance that purposes and goals be provided for each lesson and reading activity. If lessons are based upon appropriate measures of ability and interest, the instructional tasks become easier and more interesting. Such programs are enjoyable and child-centered and promote maximum development of the essential qualities of lifelong readers.

Conclusion

Many variables must be considered in the study and analysis of sex differences in learning to read. Mere knowledge of the fact that boys are generally slower than girls in learning to read is not enough. Teachers are urged to identify those factors that possibly interfere with the "boys' right to read" and to plan and implement programs that produce quality readers. Central to the entire problem is the need for more attention given to each and every individual. It thus becomes a challenge to every teacher to help the individual child develop habits conductive to lifetime reading enjoyment.

REFERENCES

1. Berko, J. "The Child's Learning of English Morphology," *Word*, 14 (1958), 150-177.
2. Fox, S. E. "Syntactic Maturity and Vocabulary Diversity in the Oral Language of Kindergarten and Primary School Children," *Elementary English*, 49 (April 1972), 489-496.

3. Gates, A. I. "Sex Differences in Reading Ability," *Elementary School Journal,* 61 (May 1961), 431-434.

4. Goldberg, S., and M. Lewis. "Play Behavior in the Year-old Infant: Early Sex Differences," *Child Development,* 40 (March 1969), 21-31.

5. Loughlin, L. J., et al. "An Investigation of Sex Differences By Intelligence, Subject-Matter Area, Grade, and Achievement Level on Three Anxiety Scales," *Journal of Genetic Psychology,* 106 (June 1965), 207-215.

6. McCarthy, D. "Some Possible Explanations of Sex Differences in Language Development and Disorders," *Journal of Psychology,* 35 (January 1953), 155-160.

7. McCarthy, D. "Language Development in Children," in L. Carmichael (Ed.), *A Manual of Child Psychology* (2nd ed.). New York: Wiley, 1954.

8. McNeil, J. D."Programmed Instruction Versus Classroom Procedures in Teaching Boys to Read," *American Educational Resarch Journal,* 1 (March 1964), 113-119.

9. Menyuk, P. "A Preliminary Evaluation of Grammatical Capacity in Children," *Journal of Verbal Learning and Verbal Behavior,* 2 (1963), 429-439.

10. Moncur, J. P. "Environmental Factors Differentiating Stuttering Children from Nonstuttering Children," *Speech Monographs,* 18 (November 1951), 312-315.

11. Moore, T. "Language and Intelligence: A Longitudinal Study of the First Eight Years: Patterns of Development in Boys and Girls," *Human Development,* 10 (1967), 88-106.

12. Nash, J. *Developmental Psychology: A Psychobiological Approach.* Englewood Cliffs, New Jersey: Prentice-Hall, 1970.

13. National Assessment of Educational Progress. *Newsletter.* Denver: NAEP, 1972.

14. O'Donnell, R. C., et al. *Syntax of Kindergarten and Elementary School Children: A Transformational Analysis.* Champaign, Illinois: National Council of Teachers of English, 1967.

15. Preston, R. C. "Reading Achievement of German and American Children," *School and Society,* 90 (October 1962), 350-354.

16. Stanchfield, J. M. "Boys' Achievement in Beginning Reading," in J. A. Figurel (Ed.), *Reading and Inquiry,* Proceedings, Volume 10. Newark, Delaware: International Reading Association, 1965, 290-293.

17. Tagatz, G. E. "Grouping by Sex at the First and Second Grade," *Journal of Educational Research,* 59 (May-June 1966), 415-418.

18. Templin, M. C. *Certain Language Skills in Children: Their Development and Interrelationships.* Minneapolis: University of Minnesota Press, 1957.

19. Wyatt, N. M. "The Reading Achievement of First Grade Boys Versus First Grade Girls," *Reading Teacher,* 19 (May 1966), 661-665.

20. Yedinack, J. G. "A Study of Linguistic Functioning of Children with Articulation and Reading Difficulties," *Journal of Genetic Psychology,* 74 (March 1949), 23-59.

SOURCES FOR FURTHER LEARNING: SECTION 2

☐ Brown, L., et al. "Do Reading Interests Affect the Child's Ability to Do Critical Thinking?" *Illinois School Research,* 8 (Winter 1972), 23-26.

☐ Johnson, D. "Sex Differences in Reading Across Cultures," *Reading Research Quarterly,* 9 (1973-1974), 67-86.

PROGRAMS TO HELP YOUNG LEARNERS

FOCUS QUESTIONS

- What strategies can be employed with kindergarten children who are likely to have difficulty in traditional first grade classrooms?
- How do children in an extended first and second grade readiness class adjust to a regular third grade class?
- What is STAR?
- What strategies can be used to focus on decoding skill needs?

Programs for Young Learners

AN EXTENDED FIRST AND SECOND GRADE
READINESS CLASS: CONTENT AND OUTCOMES

Sam Shohen □ Roslyn, New York, Public Schools

By the end of the school year a sensitive kindergarten teacher is likely to know which children will have trouble during first grade. In addition to youngsters who have intellectual limitations, and those with possible serious emotional handicaps, there is a small group of children who seem to have a social, emotional, and physical lag which might be simply described as *immaturity*. Lesser and Lazarus (*1*) use the following phrases to describe these children: *unable to function as a group, extremely dependent on the teacher, low in self-concept, fearful of new experiences, short attention span, unmotivated, easily frustrated, little islands unto themselves,* and *about average in ability, but immature.*

A Dilemma

The kindergarten teacher is well aware of individual differences and realizes that all children do not mature at the same time even though they are in the same chronological age range. In many schools the teacher has only two choices: retain the children in kindergarten for another year or move them to first grade.

Traditionally, retention for most children, regardless of grade level, has not been an effective approach for solving learning problems and for overcoming maturational lags. Unless these children are moved to a first grade class which is small in size and taught by a teacher who is exceptionally effective in differentiating instruction, they may be destined to failure and may suffer damaging experiences. Lesser and Lazarus (*1*:7B) excerpted descriptions from first grade teachers' anecdotal records of children where the failure syndrome was under way. They found:

the mouse – a quiet, nonparticipating, fearful, pallid little person;

the itch – an irritating busybody, a tattling fidgety nag;

the bumbler – a clumsy, poorly coordinated child who has problems using pencils, scissors, and other classroom tools;

the shrewdie – a manipulator, master of avoidance mechanisms, sometimes labeled "rat fink" by his peers;

the lost sheep – a child who is completely disorganized and seems rarely to know what is going on;

the loner – one who doesn't want to join in and stays on the fringe; and

the wild thing – an angry child who wants to do the opposite of what is in order and is a general troublemaker.

A Possible Solution

The kindergarten teacher does not want her children to become any one of those described above. If the teacher is fortunate she might have the choice of placing such children in a class designed to meet their specific needs and where they stay for two years before being integrated into regular third grade classes. Several school districts in Long Island, New York, have been experimenting with these classes, labeling them extended readiness classes, XR classes, readiness classes, or junior first and junior second grades.

The most comprehensive description of a highly structured XR program was made by Lesser and Lazarus. They hypothesized that ". . . children who lack readiness for first grade will evidence higher academic achievement following a two-year XR curriculum than they will following a regular first and second grade curriculum" (*1*:1). Unfortunately, after completing a carefully designed experimental study, they found that the statistical evidence did not support their hypothesis. However, a supplementary analysis revealed that ". . . language training in conjunction with perceptual motor training is important for achievement to be influenced substantially." Even though the hypothesis was not supported statistically, the authors stated that ". . . it is premature to discard the XR concept. Instead, more intensive training and supervision of XR teachers and support personnel are needed. Further investigation relating to cognitive processes and relating both to achievement skills is recommended. Also recommended are more detailed profiles of teacher-learner styles" (*1*:2-3).

The Roslyn Readiness Program

Taking a cue from Lesser and Lazarus, the Roslyn Public Schools initiated its first *readiness class* in 1970-1971. No formal experimental design was developed but the program was organized on the assumption that children lacking readiness for first grade will evidence better social, emotional, and academic adjustment to school in third grade after a two-year readiness class program instead of a regular first and second grade program.

Eight definite goals were specified for the boys and girls who entered the readiness class:

1. To develop a recognition and appreciation of the function of school.
2. To foster emotional growth as a foundation for academic achievement.
3. To develop ability to learn how to learn.
4. To insure success in academic progress.
5. To promote a positive attitude toward school.
6. To heighten self-image.
7. To develop self-sufficiency.
8. To improve interrelationships with peers and adults.

Fifteen children, ten boys and five girls, were selected for the class. Thirteen of the children (two moved from the community) were integrated into regular third grade classes. A second class was organized in 1971-1972 and was taught by a second teacher, while the original teacher worked with the third new class, organized in 1972-1973.

How Children Are Selected

Although procedures were refined during the first three years, the approach that presently is used to select the fourth class is similar to what it was for the first class. The first step involves testing the entire kindergarten population with the Metropolitan Readiness Test which is administered by each kindergarten teacher. The second step enlists the aid of part-time psychometricians to administer individually a screening battery, which consists of copying two geometric figures and drawing a person. The third step involves a subjective appraisal by the kindergarten teacher of each child's intellectual, social, emotional, and physical development.

After all the data are collected, the teacher, the school psychologist, and the principal meet to select the best candidates for the readiness class. Generally, boys and girls who fit into the following categories are seriously considered:

1. Score between the 10th and 35th percentile on the Metropolitan Readiness Test.

2. Score in category three or four (of a possible four point rating) on the perceptual-motor development part of the screening battery.
3. Score in category three or four (of a possible four point rating) on the emotional development part of the screening battery.
4. Are seen by the kindergarten teacher as possessing intellectual potential, yet appear to have a social, emotional, and physical lag which is reflected primarily in the youngster's short attention span and his inability to work exceptionally well independently.

Rarely does a child fit the above profile exactly; therefore, the teacher, the psychologist, and the principal provide a composite impression. In essence, objective data often become secondary to subjective appraisals, especially those of the kindergarten teacher who has worked with the youngster for an entire school year.

Classroom Environment

There are some similarities and differences between the readiness class and regular first and second grades. The most obvious differences are in the relative homogeneity of the children in readiness class and the small class size (never exceeding fifteen children). Furthermore, the teacher has a part-time aide, thereby providing more opportunities for individualized attention. Since the program extends over a two year period, the teacher and her aide virtually have unlimited opportunities to pace each child's program at a rate appropriate to his or her needs, growth pattern, and learning style.

Elsewhere, Shohen (2) described his vision of the appearance of an ideal first grade classroom. The Roslyn readiness classes have a similar appearance. The room is alive with things to do, things to think about, things to talk about, things to write about, and things to read. It is an extension of a kindergarten. There is a block corner, science table, a math table, tropical fish, gerbils or hamsters, and a place for miscellaneous activities. In essence, the room is filled with manipulative materials that titillate the senses. On the walls are pictures, experience charts, messages from the teacher, stories written by those children who can write, and various art objects created by members of the group. There are bookshelves filled to capacity, woodworking benches, and easels. There is much in the room, but it is not cluttered; it is alive and stimulating.

The teacher realizes she cannot always provide direct, first-hand, concrete experiences for the children. She provides opportunities for them to broaden their experience, thought, and language through pictures from books, newspapers, and magazines which offer simple, never-ending sources of vicarious experiences. Motion pictures, film-strips, slides, records, and tapes are other readily available sources.

In this stimulating environment the children are given opportunities to move, to look, to touch, to hear, to talk, to choose, and to explore feelings. There is, nevertheless, structure and routine that set limits and establish a sense of security. Rules and regulations are established by the teacher and the children. Above all, the teacher spends much time in planning the learning activities that she will facilitate.

In essence, a learning milieu is established where the teacher has an opportunity to extend the reading readiness activities of kindergarten and first grade in major areas as concrete experiences; concept development; vocabulary development; thinking skills; and perceptual-motor development. Also, the teacher is aided by special instructors in art, physical education, music, science, library, speech, and reading. Her program is not structured as highly as the one described by Lesser and Lazarus (1:18-28); it is simply an "open" first and second grade program where the class is small and relatively homogeneous. The pacing can be adjusted and individualized attention can be given where needed.

Parent Participation and Education

After the prospective candidates for the readiness class are selected, the kindergarten teacher meets individually with parents to explain the program and to give the reasons why their children were selected. When the program first started, the kindergarten teacher requested consent from parents. This practice was discontinued when many children were not placed in the program as a result of parental apprehensions. Presently, parents are informed and the program is described to them, but child placement is simply an administrative decision.

The teacher tries to involve parents as much as possible in her program. At an open house early in the school year, she meets with parents to describe her goals, expectancies, and methods of operation. She encourages the parents to request individual teacher conferences as often as they feel it is necessary and she schedules formal parent-teacher conferences at least twice a year to report on progress instead of issuing a traditional report card.

Furthermore, each of the two teachers has her own unique way of encouraging further contact with parents. One teacher encourages parents to visit her class to participate in activities at least twice a year; the other encourages parents to meet with her after school and she also visits parents in their homes.

Current Assessment

As indicated earlier, the first readiness class was fully integrated into regular third grade classes. Subjective evaluation by the third grade teachers and the principal suggested that, as a group, the children adjusted adequately and were fully accepted by their class-mates. Academic achievement, including reading ability, varied among the children. They seemed to have good self-images and were self-reliant. Objective measures were planned to evaluate these areas by the end of the school year. Furthermore, the principal became aware of several behavior problems among the third grade children; however, none was a former member of the first readiness class.

The readiness program has received universal acceptance by the parents. In telephone interviews where parents were asked to respond to the same questions, the principal received almost unanimous "yes" answers to questions such as the following:

- Does your child like to come to school?
- Does your child talk about school, other children, teachers, the work?
- At home does your child seem more self-sufficient?
- At home, does your child show more interest in school-type work (reading, writing, numbers)?
- Has the readiness program been a profitable experience for your child?

The principal also noted some spontaneous positive responses from the parents, such as the following: My child would have spent time in the principal's office or become a clown if there hadn't been such a class. He has grown up a lot. I would go any place, tell anyone how great the program is. I can't believe how fortunate he was to be in this particular class. I wish there had been a program like this when I was a girl.

The two readiness class teachers have had an opportunity to assess their programs. Both are veteran teachers with extensive back-grounds and experiences as nursery school and kindergarten teachers. It is interesting to note that the teachers differ in their overall reactions to the program. Both believe they have been successful with their children — one teacher believes success is due to the homogeneity of her group, while the other believes her children could have a better educational experience if there were "top" children in the group, thereby establishing a degree of genuine heterogeneity. Both teachers feel the classes need full-time teacher aides. Above all, they strongly urge that the label "readiness class" be dropped because they find a stigma has developed among parents, teachers, and children. They suggest the traditional terms of "first grade" or "second grade" be used, with the adjective "smaller" (number of children) applied if further explanation is necessary.

The principal believes the readiness class concept has been very successful and has recommended to the superintendent and board of education that the program be continued. The principal's reactions to the program are enthusiastic, but subjective. He would be the first to admit that success might be simply due to the competence and sensitivity of the two wonderful human beings who are the teachers; nevertheless, the results of the program are encouraging. Perhaps similar preventive programs can be established and studies undertaken to evaluate their effectiveness.

REFERENCES

1. Lesser, Irwin J., and Phoebe W. Lazarus. *Extended Readiness.* Westbury, New York: Nassau Board of Cooperative Educational Services, 1972.
2. Shohen, Sam. "A Language-Experience Approach to Reading Instruction," in T. Barrett and D. Johnson (Eds.), *Views on Elementary Reading Instruction.* Newark, Delaware: International Reading Association, 1973, 43-48.

A DIAGNOSTIC-PRESCRIPTIVE READING PROGRAM

Dorothy J. Gaither □ Los Angeles, California

For several years twenty-six schools in the Los Angeles Unified School District participated in a diagnostic-prescriptive decoding skills program. STAR, an acronym for *s*urvey, *t*est, *a*nalyze, and *r*ecord, began operation on August 1, 1970 under a three year E.S.E.A. Title III grant. The first two years were developmental and evaluative and the last year was one of full implementation of all products.

Basis for the Program

The program developed out of a need in one administrative area in the Los Angeles Unified School District to determine why the pupils in the area repeatedly scored markedly below the national average in the state mandated reading tests in grades one, two, and three. Those pupils in the disadvantaged schools scored especially low.

The counseling section of the area analyzed the results of the standardized tests to identify the reasons for the reading difficulties the pupils experienced. Results of the analysis indicated weaknesses in several areas. One major weakness was decoding skills — the pupils simply could not read the test and lacked the necessary skills for unlocking the words. As a result, a program was developed to provide a systematic diagnostic-prescriptive instructional program in the decoding skills.

Assessment Procedures

The first task of the STAR staff was to develop a diagnostic instrument in the decoding skills. In order to make the skills more meaningful and compatible with the daily instructional classroom program, the STAR staff researched and identified the skills introduced in the state adopted texts and other reading programs used in the area. The skills were placed on lists according to where they were generally introduced in the reading programs. A final list was compiled and the skills were placed on levels. Those skills that were most often introduced on a level were placed on that level assessment.

In order to test pupil knowledge of the identified skills, diagnostic assessments were developed on four levels. The levels ranged from preprimer to level three. The skill areas on each assessment were self-contained. This enabled the teacher to administer the assessment in its entirety or in parts, depending upon the capabilities of each pupil. The assessments were informally administered with no time limits involved. Evaluation was accomplished by the participating teachers and by a University of California team.

The teacher determined the level of assessment to be administered to each pupil. The decision was based upon the reading level of the pupils and not on their grade level. If an incorrect level was initially administered, the teacher gave the next higher or lower level.

Large charts delineating the skills were developed for each level of assessment. The results from the diagnostic assessments were recorded on the charts. A plus sign was recorded if the pupil marked the correct item and a minus sign was recorded if the item were incorrect. This enabled the teacher to look at the chart and group pupils according to specific skill need. The teacher then provided appropriate skills instruction.

In the second year of operation the scoring procedure was modified. To insure a more prompt and efficient return of the diagnostic assessment results and to free the teacher from the clerical work involved, the assessment format was changed for use with machine scorable answer sheets. The results were returned to the teachers in the form of a computer printout within a day or two after submission. This process enabled the teachers to provide immediate instruction in the skill disabilities indicated on the printout.

Prescriptive Procedures

The prescriptive part of the STAR program was developed during the second year of operation. The original objective of the program was to develop a diagnostic instrument; however, a majority of the teachers involved in the project expressed a need for meaningful prescription in each of the skill areas. The STAR staff, as a result of the request, developed prescriptive instructional materials. The materials were given to the teachers for evaluation as they were developed. After the materials were used and suggestions noted, the materials were returned to the STAR office. When all areas of the prescription had been evaluated by the participating teachers, they were submitted to Delwyn Schubert, Professor of Education at California State University, Los Angeles, and Jack McClellan, Administrative Coordinator of Los Angeles City Schools, for evaluation.

In the fall of 1972 the prescriptive materials were given to the teachers in the form of a supportive materials notebook. Every teacher received this notebook with all the materials that had been developed. The program was then complete and ready for full implementation.

Once the skill deficiences were identified, the teacher began an instructional program to eliminate the disabilities of the individual pupils. The program did not dictate any specific method of instruction so the activities varied from classroom to classroom. Through the use of the computer printout, the teacher was able to group children according to skill needs and prescribe appropriate instruction on a regular basis.

The purpose of the supportive materials notebook was to assist the teacher in planning a systematic, in-depth instructional program. The material in the notebook was to be used with the basal reader or other programs to provide additional instruction or reinforcement in skill areas. The materials were also used independently for skill development.

The notebook was divided into fifteen skill areas. Within the fifteen areas, prescriptive materials were provided for all of the skills that were tested on the diagnostic assessment. Each skill area was divided into six parts: 1) lesson ideas, 2) follow-up activities, 3) home study suggestions, 4) learning center activities, 5) suggestions for games and aids, and 6) criterion exercises.

The lesson ideas suggested a variety of teaching activities that could be used to introduce, reinforce, and enrich skill development. Also included was a list of Los Angeles City Schools Instructional Materials and commercial materials that could be used to supplement instruction in the skill area.

Follow-up activities consisted of a variety of meaningful practice sheets which could be used to strengthen knowledge of the skill that had been taught in a directed lesson. A section on home study contained suggestions to be sent home with the pupil to reinforce a skill that had been taught.

Learning center activities were planned for an individual or a small group. A learning center was defined as an area which could be planned to reinforce a skill that had been taught and reviewed in directed lessons. Teachers were to be sure that the pupils knew what they were to do and that they had an understanding of the skill concept before they were assigned to the area. The activities were self-directed and self-corrective.

Games and aids consisted of suggested activities that could be used to provide additional reinforcement of a skill. Workshops were held with teachers, aides, and parents so that the games and aids could be made for classroom use.

The criterion exercises were to be administered after the skill had been taught and reinforced to determine the level of skill mastery.

After using the STAR program for several years, many indications of success have been noted. One such area is in teacher attitude. Teachers have become more aware of the importance of meeting individual needs. They have recognized the importance of diagnosing and identifying the strengths and weaknesses of each pupil and prescribing instruction that focuses on individual needs. With a complete program available and with continuous inservice education, the teachers are more secure in the teaching of the decoding skills.

As a result of teacher awareness, the pupils have demonstrated more independence in decoding. This was evidenced in an interim study which indicated that the majority of pupils in the program were making steady gains in overall reading ability. Hopefully, the program will continue to produce such gains. A formal study to determine effectiveness is planned for publication.

SOURCES FOR FURTHER LEARNING: SECTION 3

☐ Botel, M., and A. Granowsky. "Diagnose the Reading Program Before You Diagnose the Child," *Reading Teacher,* 26 (March 1973), 563-565.

☐ Cashdan, A. "Reflections on the Beginning Reading Program," *Reading Teacher,* 26 (January 1973), 384-388.

☐ Cramer, W. "My Mom Can Teach Reading Too!" *Elementary School Journal,* 72 (November 1971), 72-75.

☐ de Hirsch, K., and J. Jansky. *Preventing Reading Failure: Prediction, Diagnosis, Intervention.* New York: Harper and Row, 1972.

☐ Hanson, I. "The Use of Two Language Screening Tests with Kindergarten Children," *Elementary English,* 49 (November 1972), 1102-1105.

☐ Hunt, B. et al. "Teaching Reading in an Innercity School: A Program that Works," *Reading Teacher,* 27 (October 1973), 25-28.

☐ Niedermeyer, F., and P. Ellis. "Remedial Reading Instruction by Trained Pupil Tutors," *Elementary School Journal,* 71 (April 1971), 400-405.

☐ Putnam, L., and A. Youtz. "Is a Structured Reading Program Effective for Urban Disadvantaged Children?" *Reading World,* 12 (December 1972), 123-135.

☐ Wooden, S., and T. Pettibone. "A Comparative Study of Three Beginning Reading Programs for the Spanish-Speaking Child," *Journal of Reading Behavior,* 5 (Summer 1972-1973), 192-199.

☐ Yawkey, T. "Reading Training and Rural Disadvantaged Five-Year-Old Children," *Reading World,* 13 (December 1973), 128-140.

☐ Youtz, A., and L. Putnam. "Is a Structured Reading Program Effective for Urban Disadvantaged Children?" *Reading Teacher,* 26 (March 1973), 644.

☐ Zaeske, A. "The Validity of Predictive Index Tests in Predicting Reading Failure at the End of Grade One," in W. Durr (Ed.), *Reading Difficulties: Diagnosis, Correction, and Remediation.* Newark, Delaware: International Reading Association, 1970, 28-33.

☐ Zdep, S. "Educating Disadvantaged Urban Children in Suburban Schools: An Evaluation," *Journal of Applied Social Psychology,* 1 (April-June 1971), 173-186.

PROGRAMS TO HELP DISABLED READERS

FOCUS QUESTIONS

- What premises about the reading process should guide remedial reading programs?
- How can cooperative relationships be established between schools and universities?
- What activities can be used in remedial reading programs?
- What is meant by coding?
- What are the basic steps in the coding approach?
- Is a child's improvement in reading a result of the remedial method or the child's internal motivation?

Helping Disabled Readers

A REMEDIAL READING PROGRAM WITHIN A COMMUNICATION CONTEXT

Kathryn O'Connell □ University of Wisconsin at Madison
and
Patricia Dew □ University of Wisconsin at Madison

Children who have had difficulty in learning to read are often confused about what reading is. A common characteristic of remedial readers is their failure to perceive reading as a communication process. Frequently they attend so carefully to the mechanics of reading that they miss the experience of getting ideas from print. Just as with oral language (one person talks and one listens), in written language there is a *talker* (the author) and a *listener* (the reader). Remedial readers seldom perceive themselves as listeners while reading. They are more likely to perceive themselves as puzzle solvers and to perceive reading as the solution of a series of difficult puzzles. Each unknown word is a unique puzzle and the sum of these puzzles, laboriously solved, is rarely an interesting idea or a good story.

Improving the remedial reader's efficiency at puzzle solving by teaching isolated word recognition skills will not necessarily improve the child's ability to read for meaning and personal satisfaction. The remedial reader's confusion about the nature of reading is at least in part responsible for his difficulties in learning to read; an emphasis on the bits and pieces only increases this confusion. In order to teach reading effectively to a poor reader, the teacher must help the child understand reading as a communication process. A successful remedial reading program must always present reading in its real setting — the context of meaningful communication.

Premises About Reading

Keeping reading within its natural environment of meaningful communication is one of the distinctive features of the summer remedial reading program described in this paper. This emphasis on reading as communication is based on the following related premises about the nature of reading, the process of learning to read, and the successful teaching of remedial reading.

Reading is an act of communicating. Reading is not simply a deciphering of written symbols. The author of the material has a reason for writing; he has an idea to express; he wants to communicate a message to someone. Likewise, the reader has an active purpose that joins the author's to complete the communication. The reader's intention is to find and interact with that idea or to "hear" that message.

Language and experience are components of reading. Since the medium of the communication between author and reader is written language, the reader's knowledge of the oral language has direct bearing on his reception of the ideas. Though oral and written English differ in some ways, the essential syntactic and semantic features of the two are the same. The reader's knowledge of the language directs his interpretation of the message. As he reads, for example, he anticipates certain types of words which "must be next" because of the restrictions of English syntax. For example, "The bright yellow . . ." will generally be followed by either another adjective or a noun.

The reader's background experiences similarly influence his reception of the written message. The reader interprets the ideas of the author according to his own experiences. Consider the example of a mystery story which is set in an old Victorian mansion. The author may include a detailed description of the layout of the house, but the reader's image of that house will include more than the author's description. His image of that house will be shaped both by the author's description and by his experiences inside old houses. The author counts on this ability of the reader to use his personal experiences to understand and to go beyond the written description.

Successful initial reading experiences are based on the child's own language and experiences. A beginning reader has acquired the basic patterns of his language. The child's oral communications are complete and meaningful. His experiential background and continuing capacity to experience are also rich and to be respected. By accepting the child's own language and experiences as the basis for reading materials, the possibility is created for the child to see reading as meaningful communication.

Compare the oral language of a seven-year-old child with the language content of common graded reading materials which attempt to control the language of the material in some way. Some materials, for example, control the phonic content (Kit's mitt fit.); others attempt to control the vocabulary content by manipulation of the story so that only the same 29 words are used throughout. This type of language control distorts both the language and the sense of the content. There is little relationship between the content of these controlled materials and the child's language or experiences. The notion that writing communicates would not readily be apparent to the child when reading these materials. The child can infer this notion best when the materials fit his understanding of reality; that is, when they use language and describe experiences close to his own.

Isolated drill sessions do not contribute to success in learning to read and, in fact, may make it harder for the child to develop the ability to read. The child's mastery of a skill in isolation does not insure that he will be able to apply the skill to a genuine reading situation. The child can practice the long and short vowel sounds and be able to recite these sounds perfectly for each letter symbol and still not be able to sound out all of the words of a reading selection. Or perhaps the child can sound out all words of a selection, but takes each word by itself, applies the skills, and proceeds to the next word without ever connecting the two. Language is not a collection of words but an ordered relationship among words. Isolated drilling of skills teaches the child to look carefully at each word separately. Each word is a new problem, and the relationship among the words is lost.

To be a successful reader the child must understand reading as part of a communication process. Children who have missed the communication aspect of reading have the impression that the correct recognition of each word is paramount in "reading." The payoff in true reading, however, comes only as one understands and interacts with the ideas of the author. If the child does not know there are ideas or stories in print, his calling of the words can only be rewarded by factors external to the content of the material (for example, teacher praise or peer recognition); there is no way for him to value reading as personal experience. If the child is ever to look for meaning as he reads, if he is ever to actually read, he must view reading as communication.

In order to learn to read, the child must perceive himself as a reader. Just as he needs to know that reading is a way of communicating, the poor reader must know himself as a reader if he is to overcome his reading difficulties. A good remedial reading program will therefore stress sustained reading rather than merely practice at reading skills. Only if the child actually reads (perceives ideas from print) can he change his perception of himself to include *reader* as one of his characteristics.

Testing has value only so far as it leads to actual instructional practices. The diagnosis of remedial readers frequently seems to be valued as an elaborate art form demanding careful and thorough expression. Numerous tests are given in hopes that a definite pattern or a clear picture of the reading problem will become apparent. Such a faith in tests, however, is unwarranted. Tests (standardized, informal, psychological, reading) have limitations which prevent them from providing a complete picture of the child's reading problem. An emphasis on testing is unwarranted also for the obvious reason that tests (even reading tests) cannot be used to teach reading.

Tests *do* give some information about what a child does as he reads. This information is useful, only when it is used to determine instruction that will remediate the reading difficulties.

There is no one method of teaching remedial reading. Each teacher must discover his own way of working with the children he is to teach; he must also discover which materials and approaches work best with these children. The watchwords of successful remedial teaching are evaluation and flexibility. The teacher should continually evaluate the child's response to the activities tried and be ready to adjust his approach. A second element of the teacher's flexibility is consideration of the child's own initiative and interests. Only the child can determine what materials, ideas, or activities are most appealing and most meaningful to him.

A trusting relationship between teacher and child is essential to the remedial program. Because reading occurs within a context of human communication, the child must feel he can express himself. The child must have reason to trust the adult before he can be asked to dictate a personal language experience story or be asked to interact with another author's ideas. True reading involves the child personally; such involvement can only be expected if an honest relationship exists between teacher and child.

From Premises to Program

These premises have been integrated into a program which features the cooperative working relationship between the University of Wisconsin and the Madison Public School System. Coordinating this program is the responsibility of the Director, a position held by the university professor who is in charge of the remedial reading practicum during the regular school session as well as during the summer session. The Director is aided in his work with the practicum students by three university supervisors who are usually advanced graduate students at the university. The role of the supervisor is perceived as more closely resembling that of a cooperating teacher rather than a person coming in from the university to periodically evaluate the teacher's performance.

The practicum students who enroll in the summer remedial reading program take the four credit university course for several reasons. The practicum is a required course for certification as a reading teacher in the state of Wisconsin, and it is also required for the master's degree in remedial reading. Some of the students enrolled in the program are regular classroom teachers so the amount of previous experience in working with children varies among members of the group.

A two credit seminar is offered in connection with the four credit practicum. The seminar is taught by the same professor who is in charge of the practicum and provides students with the opportunity to examine and discuss case studies of disabled readers. This theoretical and in-depth examination of different kinds of reading problems gives the students a broader perspective of the theory and practices inherent in different remedial approaches.

A second facet of this summer remedial reading program is the cooperation and support provided by the Madison Public Schools. A reading consultant from the public schools plays an active role in many aspects of the program. The consultant screens the children who are referred by classroom teachers. These children are chosen from grades one through five on the basis of reading problems and the degree to which it is felt they can profit from a summer remedial program. The reading consultant is also in charge of organizing the various materials brought from the public schools' central instructional materials center (IMC). These materials are all displayed in one room and are available for university and public school personnel to examine throughout the summer program.

In addition to these materials and the services of the reading consultant, the Madison Public Schools provides the school building with an IMC staffed by a school librarian. This cooperative effort between the university and the Madison Public Schools has been instrumental in the success of this summer reading program.

One of the objectives of the first week of the summer session is to acquaint the practicum students with various reading tests. Discussion centers around the relative strengths and weaknesses of diagnostic instruments such as the Gates-McKillop Reading Diagnostic Tests, the Spache Diagnostic Reading Scales, and other informal diagnostic surveys. The practicum students are also given the opportunity to examine the children's cummulative folders and teacher referral forms in order to determine the two or three students with whom they would like to work. Time is also provided for the purpose of planning and inspecting instructional materials.

The following six weeks of the program are devoted to working directly with the children. The first day of the session begins with an orientation meeting for the parents of the children. At this meeting, the parents are acquainted with the general format and philosophy of the program and also have an opportunity to meet with the teachers who will be working with their children. The teacher works with two or three children for seventy-five minutes each morning, Monday through Thursday. There are two teams of teachers, the first meeting with the children from 8:30 to 10:00 and the second meeting with the children from 10:30 to 12:00. The extra time and overlap are designed for preparation and conferences with the parents and supervisors. Friday is reserved for seminar meetings conducted by each supervisor. These meetings provide the opportunity for the practicum students to further examine materials, share ideas, and discuss common problems.

The practicum students are required to prepare a tentative diagnostic statement for each child after they have been working together for approximately three weeks. The purpose of this short paper is to encourage the student to ascertain each child's relative strengths and weaknesses based upon formal and informal tests and personal observations. This tentative diagnostic statement also required the teachers to make specific recommendations for appropriate instructional procedures and materials to be incorporated into their program.

The last week of the eight week summer session is spent in the preparation of evaluation and diagnostic statements. An evaluation statement is required for each student. This statement includes the child's current reading status and progress noted by formal or informal tests, a brief description of instructional practices and materials used, and suggestions for further specialized instruction. This evaluation statement is then forwarded to the child's classroom teacher.

Each practicum student is also required to prepare a diagnostic statement for one child. This project, when finished, resembles a case study. The diagnostic statement includes information regarding intellectual potential, performances on diagnostic reading tests, physical and mental health, home background, and characteristics of the child's previous progress in school. Based upon this and other pertinent information, the practicum students are asked to hypothesize about the cause of the child's reading problems and make suggestions for a future remedial reading program in terms of objectives, techniques and materials.

During the six weeks that the teachers are involved in working with the children, many things are done to ensure that the children have enjoyable and successful reading experiences which are placed within a communication context.

Many activities stem from the use of language experience stories which are dictated directly to the teacher or into a tape recorder. A language experience approach utilizes the child's own language and experiences, thus involving him directly in the communication of ideas. These experience stories are based on activities such as nature hikes, films and filmstrips, puppets, plays, or the children's ideas about animals, stories, and poems. Some children can also be involved in writing experience stories based on their reactions to different types of music. Telephone conversations provide a means of generating conversation which then can be written down in story or play format with the dialogue between the children becoming the basis for the experience story. Puppets can also be used to portray imaginary conversations and then recorded in play format.

Word banks are often utilized in connection with these language experience activities. The words that the children consistently recognize from their experience stories form the basis for their own word banks. Many word games that the teachers then design for their students to facilitate word recognition use word bank vocabularies in combination with standardized word lists.

A second type of activity revolves around the notion of reading for meaning and utilizing what has been read in a concrete manner. These activities stress purposeful reading which helps the child search for meaning as he reads. Some children are involved in treasure hunts which emphasize the need to read clues carefully in order to locate the treasure. Other children are successful in planting a minigarden and then making records of their observations. Reading directions in order to construct an object is another activity in which children are frequently involved. These activities result in finished products such as cookies, yarn wigs, hats, and light bulbs.

Play reading provides the focus for still other successful reading experiences. This activity seems to be the most successful in improving the child's concept of himself, both as a person and as a reader. Play reading appears in many formats ranging from finger and puppet plays to radio and television shows. Some children are able to read directly from commercially produced books of plays. Others can be successful in writing their own plays based on actual stories they have read. The use of creative dramatics encourages the children to express themselves as characters in the books they are reading. Tape recorders are often used to practice and record the children's parts before the plays are presented to an audience. This practice ensures the poor reader the opportunity to be successful and also frees him to become more actively involved in the dramatization of the play.

The fourth and final type of successful reading activity revolves around getting children directly involved in reading a variety of materials and then sharing them in some manner. A reading period is usually an integral part of each student's daily program with time being allotted for the selection of books. Everyone, therefore, has time to read. Motivation seems to be the key in getting these children initially involved in reading what for many is their first book. It is possible to get children actively involved in reading a mystery story by such means as reading the beginning of the story together in the school's dark boiler room with only the light of a candle. Others become interested in reading through watching films or filmstrips of the actual story. In one program, several children constructed a "comprehension bubble" which was used as the special place where they gathered to discuss the books they were reading. Sharing their reading experiences also provided the impetus for reading, especially when book reports took the form of mobiles, dioramas, puppet shows, and pantomimes.

In stressing these activities — language experience stories, play reading and reading for meaning — the poor reader transcends the puzzle-solving tasks and becomes immersed in reading as meaningful communication.

CODING: AN INSTRUCTIONAL TECHNIQUE FOR TEACHING READING TO SEVERELY DISABLED READERS

Carl L. Rosen □ Kent State University
and
Susan Tibbals □ Kent State University

Poor readers represent a continuum, exhibiting minor to severe difficulties in learning to read. Severe cases of reading disability are, in general, more often found among young male pupils in the primary and early intermediate grades who manifest complex and divergent behavioral patterns of nonresponse to orthography. Ambivalence to print is common, with interacting combinations of *stimulus-bound* and *stimulus-avoidance* behavior.

Mackworth (2) emphasizes the point that a definition of reading should include attention to "Who is reading what, in what, in what state, and for which reasons?" In the case of the severely disabled reader who has acquired meanings and language to symbolize his experience but is painfully unable to acquire the visual-verbal code, responses to print are emotionally exaggerated and overintense.

Often the rarely available and then uncertain efforts to remediate his difficulties clutter and compound his state of helplessness. The panic of adults — teachers and parents — contributes further to the overexaggeration of his so-called inability to acquire the code. Reading and learning disability teachers frequently, and in good faith, impose doctrinaire etiological and remedial predispositions. These efforts reflect their conceptual orientation to causes of such pupils' difficulties and to various models of reading. When misguided and misinformed these professionals recapitulate previously applied and unsuccessful strategies, or introduce approaches which reflect, as Spache (6) has pointed out, little if any clinical insights into such pupils' immediate psychoeducational needs.

These specialists require access to a wider range of alternative approaches for the immediate and successful introduction of such pupils to reading. They are in particular need of approaches that will unlock the psycholinguistic resources of such pupils in novel and indirect language-oriented reading experiences so that the energies, curiosities, and drives of the severely disabled pupil to acquire reading are rapidly and successfully channeled. Classroom teachers of young pupils would probably also find use for such strategies as supplements to their regular program.

In a previous paper, Rosen (5) presented a series of remedial strategies which are currently under exploration and refinement with severely disabled readers being tutored in a university reading center. This paper will describe a recently developed, unique approach involving *coding* which has resulted in remarkably satisfying and successful reading experiences for several severely disabled young male subjects.

Overview of the Coding Approach

Coding is a type of paired-associate strategy requiring the pupil to alternately reproduce familiar symbols from unfamiliar ones and vice versa. The setting is carefully prepared so that in the first experience the child observes his teacher decipher a message given to her by another pupil (or adult) by means of a key similar to the following:

a = ◯	b = ☐	c = ⬚	d = ⊟	e = ⊙	f = ⊡
g = ◺	h = ⊠	i = ⊙	j = ⊡	k = ◇	l = ⬚
m = ⬚	n = ◺	o = ⊙	p = ⬚	q = ⬚	r = ⬚
s = ◺	y = ⧅	u = ⊙	v = ⬚	w = ⬚	x = ◖
y = ◹	z = ⬚				

The context and content of the message is deliberately made rewarding and simple. Both the teacher and pupil decipher the code and share the results of their efforts, for example:

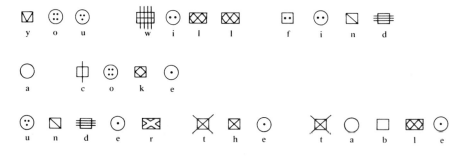

After several initial experiences with code-breaking, in which the teacher and pupil are engaged in information-processing of messages received from others, the child is encouraged to develop his own code which can be used to transmit messages to another pupil or adult. The child now engages in code-making. He may first dictate a message to the teacher and this is recorded in the familiar orthography. If he has acquired a number of sight words, these are heavily utilized for reinforcement and ease of the task in the child's construction of the message, which is then coded into the unfamiliar representational system. In no case should the child be required to tediously construct the message on his own in the early stages of the approach, unless evidence suggests that he can be successful in this task. New and unfamiliar words in his message can be immediately recorded for the child and developed for retention with modifications of the Fernald technique, sand tracing, language experience approaches, or classic remedial procedures for developing sight vocabulary similar to those suggested by Bond and Tinker (1) and Robinson (4).

The coding approach requires the child to quickly move into a regularized interaction between code-breaking and code-making involving social interaction among the pupil, his teacher, and other pupils. Secret messages between pupils are encouraged. Initially, the messages involve rewards of an immediate and primary appetitive form; but quickly their content can involve more complex two or three staged treasure hunts requiring the code-breaker to follow up on several messages which take him to different places in the room or building to find hidden messages, that ultimately lead to some final reward.

As a larger repertoire of sight words is acquired, the pupil becomes more independent in constructing his own messages, ciphering the messages of others, extracting the information, and moving about the room or building to locate from the lead message the second or even a third note. He may now begin utilizing other techniques to puzzle those to whom he wishes to transmit secret messages. He could do this by constructing messages, coding them, and then 1) deleting (cloze) nth words or nth parts of speech, 2) applying techniques of cryptography to his messages by imbedding unnecessary and confusing units (there is red a piece blue of candy green for you orange in a white purple box yellow under the brown map), 3) scrambling or distorting the order of input (the answer to this/in page six/ you will find/ of your spelling book./), or 4) stringing the presentation of words (seeifyoucanfindthesecond messagewhichjusthappenstobebehindtheteacher'schair.) The child can learn to apply many possibilities such as these for expanding and creatively developing messages beyond those within the coding technique itself. The influence of these techniques on his thinking, language, and reading abilities is discussed later.

As the severely disabled reader begins responding to print, the specialist helps him master the sight words he is accumulating by encouraging him to regularly utilize these items in message construction as well as through drills, recreational reading, tachistoscopic presentation, etc. The teacher insures that messages transmitted to the pupil are imbedded within these items and other useful words. The teacher permits the introduction of as few or as many new words as the child is able to retain, depending upon the pupil's stage of reading acquisition. On the basis of differential learning styles the teacher encourages heavy or superficial mixes of visual-auditory-oral and kinesthetic modes to the code-breaking and code-making experiences. If clinical evidence suggests that basic perceptual processes require development, for example, the child is encouraged to develop his own code and carefully depict his characters, perhaps even providing nonverbal pictorial clues, which he could copy or create. If evidence suggests that oral-aural cues require development, the inclusion of oral-mediational cues by the teacher and verbalizing by the child can be emphasized in the procedures.

Pupil strengths can also be used. If, for example, clinical evidence suggests the presence of strong visual-learning and retention modes, many new words can be acquired and overlearned through short but frequent "message-making and breaking" experiences, recreational reading, and tachistoscopic exercises.

As the pupil progresses in understanding of the representational role of orthography, gains in sight vocabulary acquisition, and develops facility in applying his language and thinking to the task of extracting meaning from such messages, he can be encouraged to produce his own stories, posters, riddles, plays, or cartoons. He can also get ideas for his own work by reading the works of others. Word decoding skills can be systematically included at first in the setting of his own specific reading vocabulary and needs, and later under more regularized and systematized instruction. At any point in this strategy, when the pupil seems to be no longer interested in or in need of the unfamiliar code as a motivational device, the unfamiliar system can be discontinued or given less emphasis.

Analysis of the Coding Approach

Coding is not a new idea to use with children and/or adults. Zim, in an interesting paperback book, describes a game-like series of activities (ciphers, invisible ink messages, and other forms of codes) that seem appropriate for many younger pupils. Bond and his students, as well as McKee (*3*), have utilized unfamiliar symbols as a means of introducing students and parents to the nature of the initial experience in the learning-to-read process. The coding approach briefly described in this paper, however, involves differentiated use of the approach over a period of time as a novel and promising introductory strategy for teaching severely disabled and immature pupils to read.

The major characteristics underlying the approach are:

1. The pupil observes competent adult readers experience difficulties in deciphering messages similar to his own problems. He participates in solving the problems.
2. The pupil is engaged in message extraction in a social context with other adults and/or pupils. Stress and anxiety, as seen in the usual reading experiences, are eliminated.
3. The pupil learns that print is a representational form of language and a useful means of communication.
4. The pupil discovers that orthography is a mechanism to impart messages. He gains mastery and familiarity over our orthography through manipulation of the familiar and unfamiliar symbols. He becomes a producer as well as a consumer of print.
5. The pupil manipulates orthography through a combination of code-breaking and code-making experiences in highly satisfying and rewarding contexts.
6. The pupil acquires a repertoire of familiar sight words which are thoroughly learned and continuously reinforced and built upon through regular exposure to decoding and encoding messages.
7. The pupil acquires a sense of personal mastery and competency as he becomes increasingly more able to independently decipher messages. He moves about collecting rewards as he breaks the code and extracts the information from the messages given to him by others. His mastery over orthography is further enhanced by his growing power to construct and transmit messages.
8. Pupils' strong modes of learning are capitalized upon and deficit modes are enhanced through various emphases on visual-motor, oral-aural, and kinesthetic experiences as the specialist applies these modalities in specific decoding and encoding experiences.
9. Pupil linguistic and conceptual abilities are capitalized upon and enhanced through both careful matching of messages to

pupil needs and abilities, as well as development of novel content in the pupil's coded messages through such approaches as cloze procedures, cryptograms, and scrambling of syntactic order. Through the manipulation of linguistic symbols, the child will learn to apply his own conceptual and linguistic structure to the reading process.

10. As the teacher observes changes in the pupil and receptivity for more systematic teaching procedures to provide word analysis skills, he may gradually reduce the time spent in decoding and encoding messages with the unfamiliar orthography and begin to emphasize more sustained writing and book reading experiences in the familiar orthography, language experience techniques, and the use of more recreational and developmental reading materials and media.

Conclusion

The coding approach is a novel and promising strategy that is presented as a new alternative for dealing with severely disabled readers. These children seem to require divergent and flexible, but clinically valid, approaches for the immediate and successful unlocking of their abilities so that they can rapidly acquire understandings regarding the reading process without failure and stress. The description of the approach is preliminary, and further refinement and experimental study is required to differentially explore the components of the approach and the specific kinds of pupil learning styles that might significantly interact with these components. The approach has resulted in remarkable responses from several severely blocked poor readers. This is of course but suggestive that the strategy might have unusual possibilities for this type of pupil as well as beginning readers.

REFERENCES

1. Bond, Guy, and Miles Tinker. *Reading Difficulties: Their Diagnosis and Correction* (3rd ed.). New York: Appleton-Century-Crofts, 1973, 311-317.
2. Mackworth, Jane. "Some Models of the Reading Process: Learners and Skilled Readers," *Reading Research Quarterly,* 7 (Summer 1972), 701-733.
3. McKee, Paul. *A Primer For Parents* (rev. ed.). Boston: Houghton Mifflin, 1968.
4. Robinson, Helen (Ed.). *Corrective Reading in Classroom and Clinic.* Supplementary Education Monographs. Chicago: University of Chicago Press, 79 (December 1953), 127-135.
5. Rosen, Carl. "Reading and the Disadvantaged: Some Psycholinguistic Applications for the Classroom Teacher," in Thomas Barrett and Dale Johnson (Eds.), *Views on Elementary Reading Instruction.* Newark, Delaware: International Reading Association, 1973, 12-21.
6. Spache, George. "Integrating Diagnosis with Remediation in Reading," *Elementary School Journal,* 56 (September 1955), 18-26.

MOTIVATION VERSUS COGNITIVE METHODS IN REMEDIAL READING

Clifford Carver □ University of Manitoba

Many reasons have been put forward to explain why a child fails in visual recognition of words. Many methods, also, have been championed as to how to remedy this defect in word recognition. Each protagonist has apparent evidence to back up his cause of failure or method of remediation. To some, word recognition failure is attributed to home relations — perhaps between mother and child. Others proffer brain damage, perceptual difficulties, slow maturation, or even multiple causes.

Remediation methods are also varied. They range from linguistic approaches, training in visual or auditory perception, multisensory methods, psychiatry, motor training or even training in crawling and eye dominance. The child's role in all this methodology is frequently ignored. He is viewed as something to which external correction is applied. Thus, the child as a dynamic decision maker often has little relevance in remedial methods.

Most facts available to the teacher regarding causes and remediation are merely superficial. There is one well-grounded fact, however, which is available to all. The fact is that only after several years of exposure to the teaching of reading is it possible to judge a child to be a reading failure — a fact he demonstrates by being unable to read. It is almost certain that by this time the child's confidence and esteem have been insulted. It is doubtful whether even the adult student could survive a fraction of the devastating failure that the retarded reader suffers. And, of course, many higher students do not survive. The longer the child has been taught without success, the greater damage to his functioning as a normal human being.

Though failing in reading, the young child continues to mature. Therefore, by the time he is judged to be retarded in word recognition, any earlier perceptual or maturational deficit may have devel-

Helping Disabled Readers

oped sufficiently to enable him to progress in learning to read. He may, however, have lost the drive, attention, and motivation necessary for utilizing his perceptual experiences. If this condition exists to any degree, then the illusions of many successful methods of remedial *instruction* is explained. In other words, the improvement made by a child could be due equally to his own internal reorganization caused by the attention he receives during remediation rather than to instruction. Experience shows that the commonest thread running through remedial education is the intensification of interest shown by the adult to the child. This factor is in contradistinction to the schools' interest in subject matter.

It was decided to test the hypothesis that child improvement in reading, following remediation, is due less to the external cognitive teaching method employed than to the child's internal motivation.

A survey using a group word recognition test (2), was carried out in a large Ontario school. The 32 most severely retarded readers were identified (mean chronological age 7 years, 3 months; mean retardation 2 years, 9 months). The assumption was made – as is made in practice – that these children needed remedial help, such help being instrumental in developing the children's reading abilities.

Two additional independent word recognition tests were administered to ensure that the most retarded readers had been selected. These were the Burt (rearranged) Graded Word Reading Test (3), and the word reading test (1) from Oxford Junior Workbook 3.

The 32 children were randomly arranged into 8 groups of 4 children each. The groups were randomly paired, one of each pair being allocated to a male or female teacher. Each pair was assigned to one of four teaching methods. The methods, designed to be as discrete as possible in content, were *cards, language, visual motor,* and *reading.*

Although each lesson was devised to be intrinsically interesting and varied, the content and times were strictly adhered to in order that each pair in a given teaching method might experience an almost identical program. If one of the pairs of groups in a method found the content of the lesson rather easy, or rather difficult, the program was still carried out. The general level of work appropriate for the 8 children in a group was evaluated each week.

The *card* method used carefully arranged visual material (letters and pictures) on cards which drew attention to letter-sound associations. No language elaboration was used, nor was the writing or reading of words allowed. All lessons were in the form of games which were used individually, in pairs, or with all 4 children in the group.

The *language* method – which was purely oral – included stories, discussions, questions, and language games. The timing, content, and general direction of activities were still controlled even though the depth of an individual child's participation could not be matched. Every child, however, was encouraged to participate and to express his feelings and ideas.

The *visual motor* method used only sensorimotor activities, such as balancing, touching, movement, left/right orientation, and manipulation. Language elaboration was not permitted in these activities; language was used only for simple instructions. Pencils and paper were used for such activities as pattern copying, but no material was used involving writing, letters, or words.

The *reading* method acted as a standard (rather than a control) to evaluate the effectiveness of the other methods. The reading group used a workbook series (Oxford Junior Workbooks) which purported to teach the child word recognition by his own efforts. Though no planning of lessons was necessary, a basic approach was used. Each child worked at his own speed. Guidance regarding what needed to be done was given initially. The children completed a double page spread which was then marked by the teacher. The child read his completed work to the teacher, corrected any errors, and continued with the next double page. No elaboration, further explanation, or questioning took place regarding the teaching aimed for in the books.

To summarize, each method aimed to give training only in that mode, thus allowing the method to be clearly defined in its supposed efficacy in improving the child's word recognition.

Weekly 45 minute teaching sessions were held, commencing in November. The children still participated in their normal class lessons during the rest of the week. Each pair of groups attended at the same time of day each week.

An important rider applying to all groups, was added to the teaching methods. It stated that a warm, friendly, and approving atmosphere was to prevail, regardless of a child's disruptive behavior or lack of ability.

The groups were taught over a period of 7 months. Retesting was carried out in January (after 5 sessions), in May (after a further 10 sessions), and in June (after a final 5 sessions).

The January retesting on all three word recognition tests ensured that the children had settled down to the routine and that progress could be evaluated during the period of January to May. This January retest also meant that the progress made by May could be judged regardless of any initial rapid progress that children often make when first receiving remedial instruction. Similarly, the June testing would show whether progress had been sustained.

After the May testing, each pair of groups was combined into the larger group of 8 children (representing that method). All teaching was carried out by a trained special education teacher who continued to use the four separate methods.

At the start of the study, the 30 next poorest readers were selected and tested from the same classes as the retarded readers. These children (mean chronological age 7 years, 5 months; mean retardation 7 months) were, on the average, two months older than the children in the experimental groups.

The results of the investigation can be summarized as follows.

1. The 32 retarded readers improved significantly at each re-testing:

   January (word recognition test 19 months; Burt, 8 months)*

   $t = 9.7$, $p < .01$.

   May (word recognition test, 12 months; Burt, over 11 months)

   $t = 13.3$, $p < .01$.

   June (Burt, 4 months).

2. There was no difference in the total improvement made by the groups (in January and May) due to the method used ($F = 6.5$; $F = .5$), to the sex of the teacher ($F = 0.4$; $F = .01$), nor to the interaction of method and sex of teacher ($F = 0.1$; $F = 1.0$).

3. The combined groups also showed no significant difference between methods in June ($F = 0.3$).

4. The improvement made by the 32 retarded readers was significantly greater in January and June than the improvement made by the class of 30 children (January, $t = 2.26$, $p < .05$; June, $t = 3.4$, $p < .01$).

5. The total improvement made by the retarded readers was not related to either their IQs (Raven Coloured Progressive Matrices) or to their original word recognition test scores.

It was concluded that the improvement of the retarded readers could not be attributed to the actual content of the teaching method. The total (June) improvements made by each method (using the Burt test) were: cards, 23½ months; language, 23 months; visual motor, 20½ months; and reading, 24½ months.

Based on the word recognition test scores, the original average reading status (against chronological age) of the 32 retarded readers and the class of 30 children was, respectively, minus 33 months and minus 7 months. By May the figures were minus 6 months and plus 3

*The Burt starts at a higher basal level than the word recognition test.

months. Due to the lower ceiling of the word recognition test, a better measure of improvement was shown by the Burt Test between May and June. The retarded readers had made an average increase of 4 months, having reduced their average retardation to 3 or 4 months while the 1½ month improvement by the class of 30 children left their status unaffected (plus 3 months).

The word recognition test median scores for the retarded readers and the class of 30 children are shown below, the final figure being based on the improvement of 4 months and 1½ months by the Burt test.

Word Recognition Test Medians

	October November	January	May	June
Retarded Readers N = 32	4 years, 5 months	6 years, 4 months	7 years, 6 months	7 years, 10 months
Class of 30 Children	6 years, 10 months	8 years, 1 month	8 years, 5 months	8 years, 6½ months

Two interpretations are possible. On the one hand, it can be argued that the 32 retarded readers would have improved in word recognition regardless of the group remedial work. Doubtless, some children would have improved; but it is difficult to accept that such sustained, above normal improvement over all groups would have taken place spontaneously. If, however, it is true that the remediation was ineffective, then it was equally so whichever method was used, including that of reading and, thus, it casts doubt on the validity of remedial education itself.

If, on the other hand, the remedial group work had some effect, then the improvement still could not be attributed to the actual content of the group work.

It was concluded that there was sufficient evidence to indicate that the children had improved because of the remediation. It was considered that this improvement occurred because many of the retarded readers were biologically able to read and that the group atmosphere and approval had released this ability by altering the child's attitude and motivation. These observations are perhaps borne out by the peripheral effects during the seven months of work. For example, many children who had apparently lacked interest in the remedial work showed great need for the emotional outlets provided by the small group atmosphere. Also, the highly disruptive behavior of 4 or 5 children gradually subsided, both in the groups and in the class. One child lost his stutter, and many were reported as showing improvement in classwork.

It is believed that this type of study needs replicating by other methods, and teachers are in ideal situations for carrying out such studies.

REFERENCES

1. Carver, C. *Oxford Junior Workbooks.* Oxford: Oxford University Press, 1967.
2. Carver, C. *A Group or Individual Word Recognition Test.* London: University of London Press, 1970.
3. Vernon, P. E. *Standardisation of a Graded Word Reading Test.* London: University of London Press, 1938.

SOURCES FOR FURTHER LEARNING: SECTION 4

☐ Applebee, A. "Research in Reading Retardation: Two Critical Problems," *Journal of Child Psychology and Psychiatry,* 12 (August 1971), 91-113.

☐ Gormly, J., and M. Nittoli. "Rapid Improvement of Reading Skills in Juvenile Delinquents," *Journal of Experimental Education,* 40 (Winter 1971), 45-48.

☐ Harris, A. "Five Decades of Remedial Reading," in L. Schell and P. Burns (Eds.), *Remedial Reading: Classroom and Clinic* (2nd ed.). Boston: Allyn and Bacon, 1972, 18-35.

☐ Kimble, R., and R. Davison. "Reading Improvement for Disadvantaged American Indian Youth," *Journal of Reading,* 15 (February 1972), 342-346.

☐ LaBudde, C., and R. Smith. "Librarians Look at Remedial Reading," *Reading Teacher,* 27 (December 1973), 263-269.

☐ Muehl, S., and E. Forell. "A Followup Study of Disabled Readers: Variables Related to High School Reading Performance," *Reading Research Quarterly,* 9 (1973-1974), 110-123.

☐ Rossman, J. "Remedial Readers: Did Parents Read to Them at Home?" *Journal of Reading,* 17 (May 1974), 622-625.

PROGRAMS TO HELP ADULT LEARNERS

FOCUS QUESTIONS

- Have gains in reading resulted from adult basic education programs?
- What are some of the elements of adult basic education programs in various states?
- How can realia be used to improve adult reading skills?
- Is there any evidence to indicate that adult reading skills can be improved by using certain types of materials?
- How can self-concept be improved through improvement of adult basic reading skills?
- How can adults be encouraged to take a share of the responsibility for improving their basic reading skills?
- How can bilingualism be incorporated into adult literacy programs?
- What are the various elements that should be considered in a model for teaching reading to bilingual adult learners?

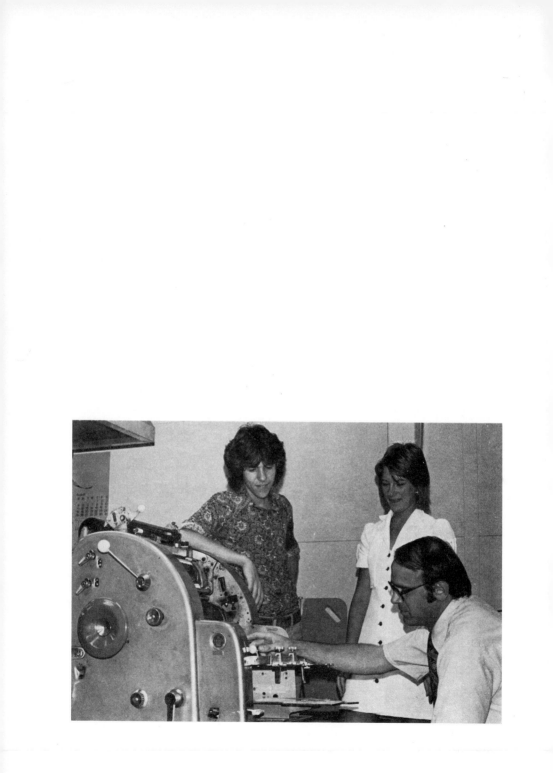

DO ADULT LITERACY PROGRAMS MAKE A DIFFERENCE?

Edwin H. Smith □ Florida State University
and
McKinley Martin □ Florida State University

Do the literacy segments of adult basic education make a significant difference in the lives of ABE students? Most adult basic education teachers would probably answer "yes," but they would note that many of the influences cannot be measured presently. There are means, however, of objectively assessing the literacy segments of ABE programs. Richard Nixon put it this way (*12*):

> What is required of the area of continuing education, especially basic education, is that it must be far more extensive than at present; it must be varied; it must be specific, yet, it must be concerned with the whole person; i.e., the total development of the individual. Merely to train a person to perform a routine or even skilled task without consideration for his total growth is giving him short term help which must be repeated continually as his job changes. This is not quality education and if we want people of quality, we must educate them accordingly. The education of adults must have long-range goals just as does the education of children and youth . . . .

Before focusing our attention on literacy programs, it is important to note the true reason for such programs. The basic objective is to change people and better enable them to cope with future change. Basic skills are but vehicles to the larger goal. To quote from a relevant study (*5*):

> They need basic instruction of a kind employers do not ordinarily provide and that their employers, with whom their connection may be casual, would not find it worthwhile to provide. At the same time, they may be unable to pay for their own instruction and indeed may be unaware of its value to them.
>
> Functional illiteracy should be recognized as a disease in a society as wealthy, as well educated, and as integrated as ours. To eradicate this disease is, in our opinion, a function and responsibility of better educated citizens in communities across the nation.

Harmon (8) offers further support to the foregoing position:

The National Advisory Committee on Adult Basic Education in its Second Annual Report (1968) states that in ABE programs in 1967

62,000 adults learned to read and write for the first time;
28,000 registered and voted for the first time;
 3,500 used their public libraries;
37,000 found jobs, received raises, or were promoted;
48,000 entered job training programs;
25,000 opened bank accounts for the first time;
27,000 became subscribers to newspapers or magazines;
 8,000 left the welfare rolls and became self-supporting;
 5,000 helped their children with school assignments.

   . . . the committee claims that "these results show that the program of Adult Basic Education has become one of the nation's positive investments in human resources."

A further look at some national highlights as given in Adult Basic Education Program Statistics (National Center for Education Statistics, U.S. Dept. of Health, Education, Welfare, 1969) shows that:

The Adult Basic Education Programs sponsored under the Adult Education Act of 1966 provided basic education to approximately 485,000 adult students throughout the United States and outlying areas during fiscal year 1969. This reflects an increase in enrollment of approximately 29,000 students, or 6 percent over the preceding year.

New enrollees represented about 56 percent of the total enrollment during fiscal year 1969, with 22 percent of the new enrollees entering the programs at the beginning level.

A total of 85,659 students were reported as having successfully completed the program through the advanced or 8th grade level of instruction. This represents a 58 percent increase over the 54,100 who completed the program through the 8th grade level during the previous year . . . .

While enrollment figures indicate the programs are reaching more students, the figures fail to tell much about the quality of the program or about the increase in basic skills competency.

During the period referred to (fiscal year 1969), the cost for an enrollment of 484,626 students was $36 million or about $75 per student. This figure appears to show that ABE is very inexpensive, but what it really shows is that the dropout rate is fantastic and is evidence that ABE programs may be ineffective.

For three years prior to 1969 (10) the costs were roughly $34 million, $26 million, and $31 million, while enrollments were roughly 377,000, 392,000, and 455,000.

Despite continuing inflation, the cost per enrollee in ABE goes down. But there is no research indicating whether the quality went up or down, or whether the cost went down because of a higher dropout rate.

Can Adult Basic Education Make
A Difference in Reading Ability?

In general, the answer is "yes," and the answer can be documented. New York, Florida, Mississippi, and Missouri are among the states where adult basic education has made a reported testable difference in the reading ability of adults. In these and other states, ABE has made a difference in the reading ability of urban disadvantaged, rural disadvantaged, older adolescents, and mature adults.

The New York State Study. The New York State Department of Education, Division of Continuing Education, conducted a two-year study of the characteristics of adult basic education students and of achievement attained in reading ability during 100 hour cycles. The findings included the following: 1) students who completed the first 100 hour cycle gained, on the average, about one-half year in reading ability, with the poorer readers making about three-quarters of a year's improvement and the better readers making about one-half year's improvement; 2) the average student who stayed through a second 100 hour cycle gained about four-tenths of a year in reading ability during the second 100 hours or an average of about a year over the two cycles; 3) the median age of the group was about thirty, with equal numbers of males and females (achievement of the sexes was about the same); and 4) the dropout rate was about 50 percent.

This was a large scale study and the samples for each 100 hour cycle consisted of over 2,000 students. It is interesting to find that achievement in terms of hours of reading instruction is about the same as that made in elementary schools (about 180 hours of reading instruction in grades 2,3,4,5,6) but is more than twice the progress made by disadvantaged children in elementary schools.

The Missouri Study. Ferguson et al. (7), offer some evidence that the literacy portion of ABE programs does make a difference. They found the average student in the Missouri ABE program gained about one-half reading grade levels for each 100 hours of participation. These findings are in accord with those of the two-year New York State Study.

Florida Migrant Program Studies. Reports on several Florida migrant programs indicated a plus for the literacy portion of ABE. The 10-week Broward County Migrant and Seasonal Worker's Program (4) did not stress reading and the test results reflect this factor. However, much emphasis was placed upon practical arithmetic and the average growth was one-half year per year. The Hillsborough

County program (9) reported an average gain in reading of close to one-half grade in two months.

The Mississippi Studies. The Mississippi studies (2) are possibly the two soundest pieces of research reviewed. They offer a model for areas that are doing an inadequate task of evaluating. In the first of two Mississippi reviews, both dealing with seasonal farm workers, the findings support our thesis that ABE does help.

It may be noted that the Aker study involved a stipend program and the dropout rate was 27.6 compared with 50 percent in the nonstipend programs of Missouri and New York. The student sample was about evenly divided by sex.

Success Measured by Grade Level

The selection of grade level as a criterion of program success in the Aker study leads to a concern with preprogram grade level distributions, postprogram grade level distributions, and the differences between the two. An examination reveals that over three-fourths (77.1 percent) of the student body came to the program with a grade level of less than 5.0 and nearly one-half (46.6 percent) with less than 3.0. Other related features of the preprogram distribution were 1) a range from 0.0 to 8.1; 2) a mean of 2.6; 3) a median of 2.7; and 4) a mode of 1.0 (more individuals — 30 — displayed a 1.0 grade level than any other single grade level score).

By comparison, nearly one-half of the participants tested out at grade levels beyond 4.0 after having been in the program for several months. Other related features of the posttest score distribution were 1) a range of 1.1 to 11.4; 2) a mean of 4.9; 3) a median of 4.5; and 4) modes of 3.1, 3.6, and 4.0.

When direction of grade-level change was considered, it was found that approximately 93 percent of the 183 individuals for whom pre- and posttest data were available, experienced some grade level advance. By contrast, approximately 6 percent recorded some loss and approximately 2 percent recorded no change at all in grade level.

Finally, to ascertain extent of grade-level advance, gain scores were computed for the 173 individuals who advanced. Most of the students gained from one to four reading grade levels during the six-month period. Fewer than 14 percent of the participants gained less than one grade level, and more than 17 percent gained about four grade levels. The mean reading gain for all students was 2.6 grade levels.

Another Mississippi Study (*3*) disclosed:

In terms of student achievement the program was quite successful. The overall gain in grade level was highly significant at the .001 level of confidence.

In seven of the eight centers from 1/2 to 2/3 of all students advanced more than 0.5 grade levels with many students advancing more than 1/2 grade levels during a six-month period. The highest level of gain was 4.1 grades. The program was also highly successful in that more than 75 percent of the participants continued throughout the course of the program.

Nearly 15 percent of the higher achieving students successfully passed the GED, suggesting that many students advance into or beyond the high school level as a result of the program.

This program was also a stipend program and the dropout rate was only 25 percent.

Other Studies. A number of other studies such as the *Garden State Family Living Experiment in Migrant Education* (*6*), *Nearad Programs* (*11*), and several of the migrant programs in Florida may have improved the literacy levels of the participants. These reports, as do many others, read well; but it is questionable as to whether anyone was being held accountable in terms of the educational improvement for the students. It is strongly recommended that all projects include respectable evaluational measures.

Conclusions

The literature reviewed has given some support to the thesis that literacy programs do help. Harman's study (*8*) reveals that many of the things achieved by the participants were not necessarily academic but that they may not have been achieved otherwise. As noted earlier, the program must be more than the teaching of the three Rs. Teaching the three Rs for the sake of teaching the three Rs has probably increased the difficulties encountered in enrolling and re-taining adults in traditional literacy programs. Irrevelancy can be considered one of the breeding grounds of illiteracy. It is important, therefore, to make sure that learning experiences are relevant to the student.

Strikingly noticeable in the review is the holding power that stipend programs manifest over the nonstipend programs. These facts easily could be misconstrued. The seasonal farm worker who receives a stipend for attendance in basic education programs would have no other way to survive while in attendance. Providing stipends may be a major factor in the success or failure of literacy in ABE programs.

It was discovered through project visits that various circumstances exist under which one may be called a dropout in many programs. There are known cases where students immediately developed the competencies they desired; i.e., passed the driver's test, got a job, and did not return for classes. This condition suggests that students do not have to attend programs from opening day to closing day to succeed. In addition, legislators and guideline writers might become more involved in understanding psychological and related needs of program participants in order that guidelines more realistically reflect what actually happens in programs.

Adult basic education has aroused the interest and concern of the general public. To continue to foster this interest, personnel representing each program should measure what is measurable, evaluate what can be evaluated, and apply accountability principles to the overall program.

REFERENCES AND NOTES

1. *Adult Basic Education: New York State.* State Education Department, 1967.
2. Aker, George F., et al. *Evaluation of an Adult Basic Education Program in a Southern Rural Community.* Department of Adult Education, Florida State University, Tallahassee, 1968.
3. Aker, George F., et al. *Factors Associated with Achievement in Adult Basic Education.* Department of Adult Education, Florida State University, Tallahassee, 1969.
4. Broward County. *Adult Migrant and Seasonal Worker Project Evaluation.* Broward County Board of Public Instruction, Fort Lauderdale, Florida, 1968.
5. Committee for Economic Development. *Raising Low Incomes through Improved Education,* New York, 1965.
6. Cross, Livingston. *The Garden State Family Living Experiment in Migrant Education.* Glassboro, New Jersey: Adult Education Resource Center, 1969.
7. Ferguson, John L. et al. *Adult Basic Education Missouri: 1965-1969.* Columbia: University of Missouri, 1969.
8. Harman, David. "Literacy: An Overview," *Harvard Educational Review,* 40 (May 1970), 226-243.
9. Hillsborough County. *Adult Migrant and Seasonal Workers Project.* Tampa, Florida: Hillsborough County Public Schools, 1968.
10. National Advisory Committee on Adult Basic Education. *Adult Basic Education: Meeting the Challenges of the 1970s.* Washington, D. C.: Department of Health, Education, and Welfare, 1968.
11. NEARAD. *A Diagnostic Developmental and Demonstration Project in the Process of Educating Adult Migrants.* Fort Lauderdale, Florida: Nearad, 1968.
12. Texas Education Agency. *Adult Basic Education, A Step in the Right Direction.* Austin: 1969.

USING REALIA TO IMPROVE THE READING SKILLS OF COLLEGE FRESHMEN

Frances Patai □ John Jay College of Criminal Justice
The City University of New York

The purpose of this paper is to share some of the materials and techniques which have been found to be successful in improving the reading and study skills of freshman college students who are deficient in those areas. It should be emphasized that deficiency in reading in no way reflects on students' general intelligence and capacity to function effectively. Students arrive at college with a broad background of experiences; they often have acquired much more than book knowledge. Teachers must respect students' insights and use their sophistication to motivate them to become involved in the learning process. The program described here begins with the assumption that students are capable of reading improvement and that the teacher's primary role is to help students to become independent learners.

Setting and Problem

It is necessary to describe the setting, in order to state the problem clearly. All students deficient in reading skills who enter a college reading program are placed in classes on the basis of scores made on the California Reading Test which they take prior to the beginning of the term. Students who score grade equivalents 10.4 and below are programed for Communication Skills (C.S.) 101. This course meets three hours a week, with the time equally divided between a laboratory where individual assignments are given and a seminar where readings and particular skills are discussed and developed. In addition, all students are required to participate in individual conferences with the teacher. The purpose of the course is to improve basic reading and study skills. Emphasis is on the areas of word attack skills, vocabulary, following directions, context clues, main idea, details, inferences, use of the library, and test taking. Some time is also devoted to outlining passages, note taking, and underlining in a textbook. In addition, students receive one hour a week of tutoring in reading.

Students who score 10.5 to the twelfth grade level on the reading placement test are programed for Communication Skills 102. This course has the same hours and format as does C.S. 101, but the emphasis is on advanced reading skills in areas such as main idea, inferences, outlining, summarizing, scanning, skimming, use of the library, speed of reading, study skills, underlining in a text, note taking from textbooks, lectures and discussions, types of reasoning, and an introduction to organization skills necessary for research papers.

The students range in age from 17 to 30, and there are usually no more than twelve in a class. All of the students come from inner-city areas which have been officially designated as poverty sites.

The reading laboratory consists primarily of software materials ranging in difficulty from simple study skills exercises to sophisticated texts read for literary interpretations. Since the students' reading grade equivalents range from below 7.0 to above 12.0, multileveled and multifaceted materials are available for use in the lab. Thus, once the teacher and the student have diagnosed the areas in which the student needs work, he can be given materials tailor-made for practicing and strengthening the skills in which he is deficient. The materials are all programed so the student can proceed at his own pace, correct his own work, score himself, and keep a record of his scores so as to enable him to see his progress. The laboratory work is carried on independently. The teacher is there as a consultant, should a student want clarification or help in selecting additional material. Students are encouraged to use the laboratory as often as necessary. In addition to the materials and texts, there is a colorful display of books and magazines where students are urged to browse and borrow books. The atmosphere in the laboratory, while task-oriented and businesslike, is relaxed, warm, and friendly, so that the teacher can give a student individualized guidance in a setting in which the student feels comfortable and secure.

The central problem in both C.S. 101 and 102 is how to help adult students learn skills which many of them view as childish — things they should have learned in elementary or high school. The problem is aggravated by the fact that many of the students have experienced more failure than success in the school situation and, consequently, associate learning activities with failure. Many associate school with teachers who are bored and indifferent and who rank students' needs low. In addition, many of the students have low self-images and do not view themselves as persons of scholastic worth. High school reading materials were of little interest to them and gave them an aversion to reading and study. Many found the subject matter unrelated to their lives or needs and, as a result, they failed to see any connection between the acquisition of reading skills and the possibility of using these skills to effect change in their lives.

Solution

Inherent in the solution of how to reach these deficient readers is the imperative that teachers get to know each student individually – his needs, problems, skills, talents, and outlook on life. This is an ongoing process throughout the entire term and it is begun by scheduling formal conferences with each student to be held at least once every three weeks. At these formal conferences, the teacher reviews the student's recent homework for signs of trouble spots as well as indications of improvement; discusses books the student is reading for pleasure; suggests other books to be read; and works out vocabulary problems. In addition, the students are encouraged to confer with their teacher anytime; as a result, numerous informal conferences (lunching together in the classroom and talking between classes) have been held. Each student's counselor is notified, in writing, about the student's progress and any problems he may experience. One woman student, who was not doing as well as expected, was found to be beset with troubles with her two small children. The counselors were able to restructure her work load to relieve her situation.

In addition to the help offered by the language laboratory and the individual conferences, students were encouraged to take one hour a week of free private tutoring. The tutors were assigned specific tasks on which to work with each student during the tutoring session so that specific weaknesses could be strengthened. In this manner, each student had an individualized prescription designed to meet his specific needs.

Through emphasis on providing student feedback, the students were enabled to participate in the design and improvement of course techniques and materials used. The ongoing evaluation, in which the teacher spoke little or not at all while the students articulated their suggestions and critical comments, was of great help in developing student pursuit of independent learning, while the teacher served as advisor.

Student complaints that texts were not relevant were met by using current materials at an appropriate level of difficulty – news reports, newspaper and magazine articles, texts of current protest songs, controversial television programs and motion pictures, and modern plays such as *Don't Bother Me, I Can't Cope* and *Ceremonies in Dark Old Men.* At one point, prior to the presidential elections, a political rally was organized at which speakers with three different political philosophies presented their views. When students saw that the material they were reading was pertinent to their problems and relevant to their contemporary urban life, the result was increased motivation and intensified interest. By using realia almost exclusively, students were able to make the connection between mastering reading skills and finding answers to their felt needs. They were eager to find out more about corruption in city and federal government — a subject they had been exploring in the news media. Spontaneously, they would bring to class a newspaper article pertinent to the subject. Having gotten the main idea and supportive details, they would perceive inconsistencies, contradiction, ambiguities, the use of emotionally charged words, and substitution of opinion for fact.

A variety of material from the news media was used, with emphasis placed on the acquisition of the skills most essential to immediate success; for example, word attack skills, improvement of sight vocabulary, grasping the main idea, recognizing important details, and understanding the author's inference.

Because these students often had experienced failure in previous learning situations, materials were first presented at a level where they could experience success. Thus, the students came to *expect* success in reading, which became self-fulfilling; and they acquired a self-image of being able to master skills, complete their homework successfully, pass tests, and understand inferences. In order to reinforce this attitude, students were presented with a series of short-term goals attainable in one lesson. Each goal, stated as a question, was written on the blackboard.

Before the students perused the reading matter of the day (usually newspaper articles), a list of those words which could be assumed to be new and unknown to them was written on the blackboard with brief explanations, and the particular kind of reading tasks required by the material were clarified.

Response to homework assignments was satisfactory because the assignments were given for every class session and were always marked and returned to each student with specific comments about his individual strengths and weaknesses. The assignments were reviewed with each student. They were kept brief and consisted of concrete questions, such as, "What draft reforms does Margaret Mead propose?" "What three solutions are presented to help ex-addicts get jobs?" "List three statements in the article that are not supported by specific evidence, examples, and details."

Sample Lessons

Because of student interest in the forthcoming presidential election, a political debate was organized as a lesson in note taking and listening skills. Speakers were invited from the Republican and Democratic Parties, as well as the Socialist Workers' Party, to campaign for their respective candidates and then respond to student questions. The entire program of speeches, questions, and answers was recorded and videotaped so that students could listen later for reinforcement and clarification, should a disagreement arise. Prior to the rally, students had a lesson on words frequently used in politics to familiarize themselves with terms such as *rhetoric, isolationist, conservative, liberal, chauvinist, radical,* and *reactionary.* They were asked to take notes during the speeches in order to answer the following questions: 1) What was the main idea of the Republican speaker's talk? 2) What was the main idea of the Democratic speaker's talk? 3) What was the main idea of the Socialist Workers' Party speaker's talk? 4) Cite three examples of the speakers' use of emotionally charged words. 5) List one example of *fact* and one that was the speaker's *opinion* for each of the speakers.

The students visibly enjoyed the rally and came prepared with specific questions on topics such as Viet Nam, abortion, and inflation. After the rally, class discussion focused on answers to the questions and student and speaker biases and ways in which correct and accurate evaluation of what is being said can be influenced by one's own point of view. Student feedback showed that they were discovering for themselves what it means to listen effectively and assess contrasting views.

Some reinforcement activities which the students pursued included writing letters of protest demanding action on certain items, using newly-acquired political vocabulary to give a political speech of their own, bringing in news items and editorials on the one subject from several sources, discussing differences in various editorial approaches, and reading and analyzing many political speeches. In this manner, reading was integrated with the other communication skills of writing, speaking, and listening.

Through analysis of a political speech by Governor Wallace (6) the students learned to read for the main idea; to find important details; to distinguish fact from opinion; to identify ambiguous statements; to recognize emotionally charged words and the "just plain folks" approach; to discover the author's purpose and biases, observe some assumptions he made, and to decide whether to accept those assumptions as fact.

A similar lesson using a McGovern speech (4), provided students with an opportunity to discover certain effects the Senator tried to achieve and the linguistic devices he used to achieve his purpose. Students then examined and compared McGovern's purpose and that of other politicians.

An article by Israel Shenker (5) on good political language (iron curtain, silent majority, generation of peace) and bad political language (bloviation, let me make one thing perfectly clear) led students to pursue vocabulary building on their own when they saw how language can clarify or obfuscate meaning.

Evaluation

How well does this approach accomplish the general and specific objectives? Evaluation of the course was a continuous and ongoing process in which both teacher and student participated. Students were able to diagnose their own progress in specific areas and to see how the learned skills helped them in other subjects. Using student feedback, the teacher was able to utilize this input to alter and restructure the class techniques and materials when necessary.

The thrust of the reading program was the enhancement of the entire personal development of the student. Therefore, objective tests can only partially measure student progress. In addition to administering the California Reading Test at the end of the term, continuous subjective evaluations were made by observing the influence of the course on student skills, attitudes, and personalities; scholastic progress in other subjects; participation in discussions and debates; speaking vocabulary in use everyday; and growth in student awareness and ability to interpret the surrounding environment.

Other specific questions were: Can students determine the meaning of unknown words by using context clues? Can they work independently and effectively with dictionaries, encyclopedias, and Roget's *Thesaurus*? Can they answer factual questions accurately? Do they grasp cause and effect relations and sequence of events? Can students appraise their own progress by looking through their individual folders and interpreting test results, homework samples, and notes on books read? Are they reading newspapers and books on their own? Can they distinguish fact from opinion? Can they summarize, outline? Are they aware of the author's point of view and competence? Can they use catalogs and reference books in the library? Can they apply their reading and study skills to tasks in other subject areas? A final and perhaps most important criterion is, do students enjoy the experience of reading?

A Final Word

The maxim that students learn when they are motivated has been repeated for many years. Adult students who have problems in the basic reading skills, however, seldom are given material which is meaningful to them. Teaching reading skills through use of various realia, particularly newspaper articles, may help to solve motivation problems. When presented with reading matter that relates to his frame of reference, the adult college student from an inner city background who is intelligent and sophisticated in many areas, realizes that the written word can contribute to his life experience and help him solve some of his problems. Pertinent materials will stimulate the student to read more and read independently; gradually he reads competently and effectively in other college subject areas; and ultimately, he achieves the capability of using the written word as a tool to attain individual goals.

REFERENCES

1. *A Guide for Teachers of College Reading.* New York: Office of Academic Development, The City University, 1970.
2. *A Teacher's Guide to Teaching Adult Basic Reading.* Albany: The University of the State of New York, State Education Department, Bureau of Continuing Education Curriculum Development, 1968.
3. Bossone, Richard M. (Ed.). *Teaching Basic English Courses.* New York: Van Nostrand Reinhold, 1971.
4. McGovern, George. "My Stand," *New York Times*, April 25, 1972, 26.
5. Shenker, Israel. "The Latest Word on the Passing Lexicon of Politics," *New York Times*, April 12, 1972, 31.
6. Wallace, George. "Why I Run," *New York Times*, March 18, 1972, 24.

TEACHING EDUCATIONALLY DISADVANTAGED ADULTS TO READ: A PILOT STUDY

Thomas R. Schnell □ University of Missouri at St. Louis

Because of this author's concern that adult education has not been paid the proper attention in terms of development of programs for aiding educationally disadvantaged adults and in terms of research related to such programs, an action research study was developed. This four month study, involving subjects from a black ghetto area of St. Louis, Missouri, was intended to improve the reading skills of semiliterate adults, and to provide information regarding the influence of certain instructional materials on reading achievement.

Two significant factors operated in the second part of the study. The first was the constant suggestion by most publishers that the way to solve reading problems was to provide these semiliterate adults with books written at a very low difficulty level but at a high interest level. The second factor emerged from a study by Sticht and others (1). The purpose of that study was to determine functional literacy levels for selected Army jobs into which many lower aptitude men were assigned. In the study, the authors examined readability levels of three job manuals (cook, general vehicle repairman, and supply clerk) and the relationships between a man's reading ability as measured by standardized tests and his performance on these job reading tasks. Findings indicated that the reading difficulty levels of the materials exceeded the average reading ability levels of the men by 4 to 8 grade levels, yet job performance of the men was generally adequate. Sticht and others drew two major conclusions: 1) any readability formula scaled on grade school material and children's comprehension of that material is not useful with adult-type materials, and 2) that the apparent motivation of a job-oriented task may be an extremely important factor. At any rate, these items were the primary bases in the development of this author's study.

Statement of the Problem

The purpose of this study was to determine if intensive teaching of reading skills to semiliterate adults would result in significant improvement of their reading skills and, if so, to determine whether the materials used for instructional purposes significantly affected the improvement. Also, the students' feelings about the program were assessed to see if any interaction existed between instructional materials and self-perception related to improved reading ability.

Hypotheses

The study resulted in the statistical treatment of several research hypotheses which were derived from the following questions:

1. Among semiliterate adults, does the use of high-interest low-vocabulary instructional materials provide greater gains in reading than the use of materials encountered frequently in daily activities?
2. Does the use of either of these types of materials result in more positive feelings about the instructional program?
3. Does the type of instructional material used interact with the students' feelings about the program?

Procedure

The subjects of this study were 50 black adults, male and female, ranging in age from 24 to 53 years, who lived in a federally-sponsored housing project in St. Louis, Missouri. They had volunteered for participation in the literacy program and entered with high degrees of enthusiasm. None of the adults had a high school diploma or its equivalent, and only 29 of the 50 had ever attended high school. The actual range of educational levels (years of schooling) was from grade 3 through grade 10. From this original group, two subgroups of 25 adults were selected randomly, before any testing or instruction took place, and were arbitrarily designated as Group A and Group B.

After assignment to a group, each subject was given Form A of the Gray Oral Reading Tests, an individually administered reading test which reports results in terms of grade level equivalents. Results of this test were used for two purposes: 1) to provide base line data for comparison at the end of the program; and 2) to provide information about instructional materials to be used with members of Group A, materials which were to be at or near the members' reading levels. Of importance to this pilot study was the finding that the two groups were relatively similar in terms of their reading ability prior to any instruction. Group A had a mean grade equivalent of 4.7 with a range from 3.0 to 8.3, while Group B had a mean grade of 4.8 and a range from 3.0 to 8.8.

Table 1

Pre- and Posttest Means of Groups A and B
on Gray Oral Reading Tests

Group	Pretest Mean	Posttest Mean
A (high-interest materials)	4.7	5.6
B (functional materials)	4.8	6.4

After gathering the preliminary information, a program of instruction was developed for each group, but not for each individual within the group. Each group met for one hour, three times per week, for four months. During these instructional periods (Group A from 9:30 a.m. to 10:30 a.m. and Group B from 10:30 a.m. to 11:30 a.m.), the instruction was presented in as nearly identical a way as possible. A reading skill was introduced, discussed, practiced, and then reviewed. The subjects then worked independently on those skills. The subjects in Group A worked in high-interest materials at or near their reading grade level, as established by the pretest. Subjects in Group B worked in materials chosen for their utility in daily activities (daily newspapers, magazines, driver's license forms, welfare forms, and job application forms). No particular attention was paid to the readability of these materials; however, it is probably safe to assume that nearly all of the materials were at a difficulty level higher than the mean reading grade level of the group.

Following the instructional period of four months, all subjects were administered Form B of the Gray Oral Reading Tests to determine whether any gains had occurred (see Table 1). Also administered was a questionnaire designed to assess the subjects' attitudes about the program in general and their opinions as to how much the program had helped them.

Results

The data gathered in this study related to reading achievement were treated statistically to determine if significant gains or losses had occurred from pretest to posttest, and to determine whether such changes were significantly different (at the .05 level) between groups. The statistical technique employed was multiple linear regression which yielded an F-Ratio statistic.

Table 2

Statistical Results of Gain Scores for Groups A and B

Hypothesis	R^2 Full	R^2 Restricted	Degrees of freedom Numerator	Degrees of freedom Denominator	F	P
1. There will be a statistically significant difference between pre- and posttest means for both groups	.218	.00	1	48	13.631	.00019
2. Group B gains will be significantly greater than Group A gains	.781	.699	1	47	17.568	.00012

The results of the attitude questionnaire were examined to determine whether one group had a more positive feeling about their program of instruction than did the other group, and to discover whether attitudes as measured by the questionnaire interacted with reading achievement.

The results indicated the following: 1) Both groups showed gains in reading achievement from pretest to posttest. 2) Group B, using materials not graded in difficulty, had significantly greater gains than Group A. 3) Questionnaire tabulations showed that Group B had more positive feelings about their program of instruction and the gains they thought they obtained from the program; however, the positive feelings were not found to have a statistically significant interaction with reading achievement.

Discussion

Based on the above findings, it appears that the type of instructional program carried out with both groups of adults in this study was effective in producing an increase in reading achievement. The length of class periods (one full hour) and the number of sessions (48) seemed to suit the situation quite well. Also, having the classes in mid-morning seemed to be a positive factor in the program (although there is no way to substantiate that claim).

The findings of this study seem to further bear out those of Sticht and others, namely, that the discrepancy between reading achievement levels and readability levels is not nearly so important with adult readers as is their interest in the materials and their task motivation. The fact that both groups in this study showed gains indicates that planned, systematic instruction in reading can pay dividends to the learners involved; however, it also seems to show that no specially developed instructional materials are necessary.

In terms of motivation and self-perception of program value, the results of the questionnaire showed clearly that the adults in Group B had more positive feelings about what they learned in the program. It seems attributable to the relevance of their daily "survival" activities to their instructional materials. The Group B students perceived a need to learn to read want ads and job forms, while Group A participants were presented only with the need to learn to read in general, which may have reduced their overall motivation and subsequent reading gain.

Summary and Recommendations

This study, carried out with semiliterate black adults, was intended to determine whether systematic reading instruction can produce gains in reading achievement, whether instructional materials used can result in differences in gains between groups, and whether materials used can affect perceptions of program value. The results supported all of the above. Based on the results, the following recommendations are made: 1) Systematic adult education reading programs should be developed to help alleviate the existing literacy problems. 2) Instructional materials used in such programs should be closely related to daily reading activities, even if their readability is higher than the reading achievement of students.

In conclusion, it appears that increases in reading performance, with the type of population studied here, are more closely related to interest and applicability of instructional materials than to the readability of those materials. Further research and replications with different populations should be done to more accurately reveal the validity of these findings.

REFERENCES

1. Gray, William S. *Gray Oral Reading Tests, Forms A and B.* Indianapolis: Bobbs-Merrill, 1967.
2. Sticht, Thomas G. et al. "Project Realistic: Determination of Adult Functional Literacy Skill Levels," *Reading Research Quarterly,* Vol. VII, No. 3 (Spring 1972), 424-465.

PROMOTING LITERACY THROUGH
THE ADULT SCHOOL PROGRAM

Elinor Tripato Massoglia □ North Carolina Central University

The main purpose of this paper is to explore the potential of bilinguality as a component of literacy programs offered under the aegis of adult education. Literacy is defined in a broad sense to include oral language facility and the ability to read, write, understand, and integrate information.

This presentation considers two basic questions that are encountered in present or projected bilingual undertakings: 1) How can one help an individual improve his communication skills in an effective, efficient, and humane way, respecting the old culture while bringing in the new? and 2) Who should be the gatekeeper of the method and material to which the adult learner is exposed?

The ABC Model for Promoting Literacy Through Bilingual Adult Education Programs (model shown in Figure 1) is a step-by-step process model presented as a conceptual framework for the delivery of literacy training through bilingual adult education. The sequence is not designed to establish preferred guidelines for the development of such programs, but to generate ideas for further consideration and exploration.

Commonality of Terms

Educational jargon often creates a terminological muddle. It is, therefore, both necessary and appropriate to describe relevant concepts as they are used here.

The adult education program envisioned here is carried on by established educational organizations. Programs may emerge from the parent institution, or they may develop cooperatively in response to the needs of any other organization in the community that provides training for its members.

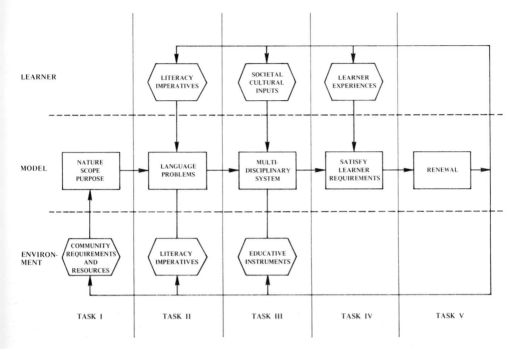

Figure 1. ABC Model for Promoting Literacy Through Bilingual Adult Education Programs

Course-contact for the program may take place during a regular school day, in the evening to accommodate adult availability, or on-the-job. Behavioral objectives may be met in the group setting of a classroom, in a learning laboratory of the parent institution, or in any other locality where maximal learning can take place. Sponsors may extend instruction into the community to promote the learner's progress in literacy and job-related and community-related skills.

The participating adult is any person beyond the age of legislated compulsory education who engages in purposeful, systematic learning in contrast to his random, unexamined experiences in everyday living.

Bilingual education operates when two languages are used as media of instruction: the learner's mother tongue and English. The target population receives the same training and takes the same courses as other students might take in traditional situations. Added, however, is the study of the history and culture associated with the vernacular.

To answer the two questions posed earlier, the following five tasks are considered:

Task I.   Determining the scope, nature, and purpose of the bilingual program.

Task II.   Identifying, defining, and limiting the language problems that ethnic groups bring to the learning situation,
so that components identified lend themselves to manageable analysis and curriculum planning.

Task III.   Devising an interdisciplinary, multimedia system readily adaptable to the concerns of different ethnic
groups.

Task IV.   Meeting the needs of mature students with a range of
educational backgrounds, personal experiences, and
abilities.

Task V.   Incorporating provision for a continuous "organizational renewal" process (*12*) that will improve the
functions in the internal system and enable it to adapt
to future changes in its external environment.

Task I: Determining the Scope, Nature, and Purpose of the Program

The word *program* is defined as "a list of events, pieces, per-
formers, speakers" in a plan of procedure. The adult educator com-
monly uses this flexible term to reflect the wide range of learning
activities that he offers.

Adult education programs typically emerge in response to specific needs, for the adult educator purports that he will teach
whatever the student wants or needs to know. Implicit is the notion
that a program is expansive, flexible, and based on the needs and
interests which students themselves express or which they can be led
to recognize. To this end, the learner becomes an active member of
his program-planning team.

The concept of bilingual programs in adult education opens to
educators a veritable virgin field for exploration and innovation.
Generally speaking, research carried on with the adult learner is
"abysmally small" (*17*), a condition ripe for change. Recent legisla-
tion (*3,15*), provided funds for the formal language instruction of
mature students who have inadequate skills of communication in an
English-dominant environment. With an open system and available
funds, what else is needed? Ideas, the avenue to action!

The adult educator's port of entry to bilingual education may be
through the language-conversion of viable programs already functioning in the English language. If modified offerings are structured to be
responsive to the needs and desires of the adults they are intended to
serve, adult participation may be assured.

Assuming that the adult educator has English-dominant programs
that can be translated into other languages, who can operationalize
the task? One can turn to colleges and universities which are experi-

encing a "crisis in foreign language education" (*16*). The chances are great that some of these institutions might be receptive to a much-needed shot of academic adrenaline. Students of foreign languages can be drawn into the adult bilingual educational enterprise, a move that may reappraise, reaffirm, or recharge the demand for foreign language study.

The decrease in foreign language enrollments during the past decade has resulted in decreased language requirements in colleges and, consequently, fewer course offerings. Ironically, this situation exists at a time when there is a scarcity of adequately prepared teachers to meet the challenges of bilingual education. It appears that there has been a communication deficit somewhere.

Since Title VII of the Elementary and Secondary Education Act was passed in 1968, a cumulative total of $86,303,251 has been invested in HEW programs (*7*), reaching 109,533 participants. More than $33 million were appropriated for the 1972 fiscal year alone. Adult educators and foreign language teachers, by combining forces and resources, can create new imperatives for learning.

Comprehensive guidelines for planning and implementing bilingual programs are given by Andersson and Andersson (*1*), who hail language and cultural pluralism as an "untapped national resource." They emphasize the "ultimate product," people – a concept that is explored with full respect for the identity and worth of the learner.

Appelson and Semple (*2*) describe English and citizenship programs for the foreign born. Brennan and Donoghue (*5*) guide adult learners toward biculturalism through individualized programs of job and community-related activities, planned and implemented within a bilingual, bicultural context. Gutierrez (*9*) promotes the development of bilingual specialists in professions and occupations. Wissot (*21*) provides a framework for expanding the high school English-as-a-Second Language program by utilizing the total educational resources of the school in a climate that fosters bilingual learning.

Any program developed along these lines becomes much more than the teaching of the vernacular and English. Established is a learning environment that demonstrates the importance of both languages as tools for learning. It is possible for the adult to effectively and efficiently develop communication skills necessary to function, compete, and operate in his pluralistic society. In a humane way, the old culture is retained and respected while bringing in the new.

As a community considers the purpose of bilingual education in its environment, one point seems clear. To become a realistic goal, bilingual education must commit itself to a total rejection of ethnic separation. A program that is well-designed, organized, and integrated into the life of the community serves all segments of that community. Its services are never *imposed on* members, but are *composed by* members as they define indigenous interests and needs. If bilingualism is truly an untapped national resource, then it is reasonable to assume that it is a desirable condition for all citizens.

Task II: Identifying, Defining, and Limiting Language Problems

The second task to be accomplished is that of identifying, defining, and limiting the language problems that ethnic groups bring to the learning situation. Components described lend themselves to manageable analysis and curriculum planning.

A study committee, organized to explore the potential needs in a particular community, can be the catalyst for creative action. It is wiser to work through existing patterns of education-community leadership than trying to work through newly created or separate entities of innovation. "Piggy-backing" on an already viable education-oriented group, such as the local PTA, may energize action. Involving commercial enterprises may ensure the success of the program. It can be conjectured that any increase in the learning power of citizens may increase their earning power, the arousal point of economic involvement.

The components of a particular community will vary, but the following information may help to define bilingualism in that community:

- A description of the people, languages, and socioeconomic levels existing in the environment.
- The occupations and job roles of the citizens.
- Potential literacy needs of the target population.
- Names of persons and/or organizations interested in promoting the development of a bilingual program, or pursuing its offerings for self-interests.

Program planners examine all aspects of possible offerings to prepare potential learning activities for differentiated instruction, goals, standards, techniques, and materials in harmony with the potential abilities, aptitudes, and requirements of the adults who may participate. Inputs to the system are derived from the external environment: what people do at home, at work, and at play.

Every effort is made to determine the *literacy imperatives* (*13*) of the community. The author has coined this term to describe any language-learning need that emerges from the inner motivation of a particular individual. A literacy imperative demands more than individualized instruction; it requires learning activities specifically structured to meet a high-priority language objective.

Literacy imperatives may exist as a need at the lowest level of survival or safety — such as reading and understanding signs that warn the adult of danger — to the highest level where, for example, the non-English speaking professional may wish to expand his practice to include English-dominant clientele. The communication is prepared in terms of its content; language-assignation is the learner's choice. In any case, the objective is an enabling skill related to reading, writing, or speaking, or a combination of these facets of the language arts.

Tyler (20) describes needs in this sense as the "gap between what is and what should be." The present discussion stresses what the learner wants it to be.

This is not to imply that the learner always knows what is best for him, for research indicates that adults are often unaware of many of their most important needs (11). The viewpoint focuses on the unique features of the particular situation for which a program is being developed. The client, or user, need is the basis for identifying problems and establishing potential priorities.

Community involvement is crucial. Citizens who have attained the highest limit of education and those who have had no formal education create a network of communication to set in motion the wheels of action. Through radio, television, social agencies, churches, and political and business groups the community defines literacy imperatives that form the bases for its bilingual education program. As Plato once stated: "Whatever is honored in a country will be cultivated there."

Task III: Devising an Interdisciplinary, Multimedia System

The third task requires the development of an interdisciplinary, multimedia system readily adaptable to the concerns of different ethnic groups.

Practitioners in every discipline do some soul searching by asking: What part do we play in the process that takes place as educators proceed to make and carry out language decisions? What can our discipline give to a bilingual education program, and what can we get from it? Responses may vary with academic differences in theory and practice, but there are several seeds of promise that may germinate and reach fruition on the open market. Below is a thumbnail sketch of some potentialities.

Sociology. Through cooperative planning between professors of sociology and adult education programers, compatible joint objectives are accomplished. Students of sociology have a unique opportunity to study the concept of bilingualism explored as the interaction of two or more linguistic systems in which societal members function alternately, to a greater or lesser degree.

As students interact with adults engaged in literacy training, the exchange includes notions related to culture and society: how to be productive, comfortable, and live in a pluralistic society; and how members can contribute to that society. Not only is a college student functioning in a competency-based sociology course, but from his "success" emerges another adult learner who has developed communication competencies within the framework of a sociological phenomenon.

Psychology. Students of psychology provide valuable information concerning the principles of adult learning, and the attitudes and personality traits that affect individual language preferences. Psychology students also help allay fears and doubts pertinent to the adult learner's new environment and possible problems of adjustment.

Through current research in the field, the student substitutes real-life study for the ubiquitous college course required term paper. By involving himself in the bilingual program, the professor of psychology injects into his course a fluid flow of individual study projects for student self-selection. Knowledge gained is fed into the bilingual education system to be examined, further explored, or assimilated.

From efforts such as these, the adult literacy learner reaps a rich harvest. He interacts on a one-to-one basis with people interested in him as a person, and concerned about behavioral changes that do something to him as they do something for him — a humane approach to cultural alteration.

Tests and Measurements. As the student of tests and measurements draws in-the-flesh and living-color statistics, the adult learner receives feedback concerning his own language progress. The tester and the tested learn together; one makes an assessment, and the other makes an adjustment in the light of that assessment. Both learners thus become more responsive to active knowledge and personal relationships.

Music and the Arts. A community resource list compiled by the local allied arts group is a veritable treasure chest. Multiethnic cultural objects, costumes, songs, dances, and works of art are readily shared with individuals and groups in the community. Teachers in the local schools utilize services to bring new life into the mainstream of education. Individuals who share their talents reap the reward of greater pride in self-identity.

Professors of Reading. The reading specialist utilizes his expertise to articulate literacy efforts at all levels on the continuum. His students of reading function as aides in the adult bilingual program. For example, as students learn how to teach word attack skills, the adult learns with them. Each has something to give; each has something to get. Aides who do not possess foreign language ability work with English language lessons, or provide other necessary services.

Drawing from these and other appropriate mentors, the bilingual education program is an all-out community effort. By identifying, collecting, storing, and disseminating a wealth of prescriptive materials adaptable to the unique personality and past experiences of the adult learner, the adult educator facilitates learning activities that his student can get through no other source.

Task IV: Meeting the Needs of Mature Students

How can the literacy needs of the mature learner be met in an effective and humane way? Adult educators may gain insight from Hutchins (*10*) who proposes that contemporary society become a learning society by setting free the mind of every man, enabling him to reach his fullest potential during a lifetime of living and learning. In making provisions for the development of its members through deliberate, organized efforts to help people become intelligent, the learning society becomes a humane society. The assumption is that the final decision to change, or not to change, remains the right of the individual.

In like manner, the ABC Model attempts to free the learner. He is placed in a somewhat autonomous role, where his adult inclinations tend to be more comfortable. He is provided with choice alternatives toward biculturalism that he may select with freedom in defining and charting his own goals, and in deciding how best to pursue them.

Three choices are open to the adult in the selection of language preference for initial instruction:

Alternative A is the learner's choice. He has demonstrated bilingual balance as a positive or negative condition. Positive bilingual balance enables the adult to operate with equal facility in the vernacular and English. Negative bilingual balance indicates that literacy deficits of a common degree exist in both languages.

Alternative B indicates vernacular-dominance; preferred instruction takes place in the learner's mother tongue. English is taught as a second language.

Alternative C indicates English dominance; preferred instruction takes place in English. Second language study is offered.

Through bilingual education, the adult expands his potential as a person so that, in effect, he becomes as many different persons as languages he knows.

A climate of independence is fostered when the adult learner enters the program. He is guided to bring into focus past experiences, ideas, and goals that may contribute to present objectives. Through interviews, discussions, and questionnaires presented for reflection during an informal period, he cuts the key to his literacy training. A cyclic, developmental sequence is identified in Figure 2.

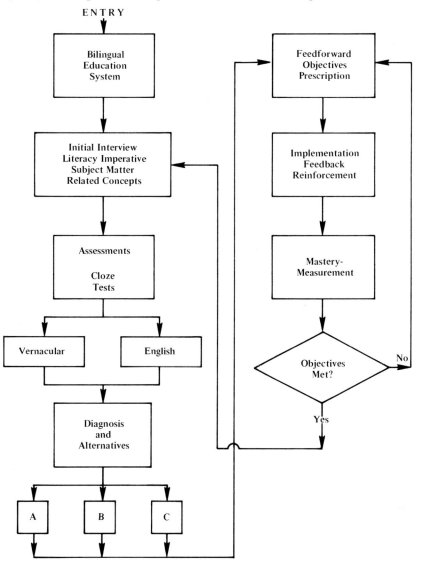

Figure 2. Flow Chart Depicting the Cyclic Process of Renewal

The learner gains entry into the bilingual education system. The initial interview provides him with information and orientation to the learning environment. The interviewer has bilingual balance, a condition that enables him to operate with equal facility and proficiency in the learner's mother tongue, or in English. Through informal conversation, answers to the following questions are sought:

- Is the learner bilingual and, if so, to what degree?
- What is an estimate of his present literacy level?
- What literacy imperatives are expressed by the learner?
- What information can be used in the preparation of diagnostic tests for entry-level assessment?

Assessments are made through a testing program tailored to the learner. The cloze procedure (*19*) is among the instruments used. Based upon information obtained during the initial interview, cloze tests (*14*) are prepared to establish the learner's level of understanding of 1) the vernacular in oral communication, 2) the vernacular in written communication (if literate), 3) English in oral language, and 4) English in written language (if literate).

Diagnosis is a joint effort on the part of the instructor and the student to determine a point of departure for initial language activities. Through careful interpretation of the cloze test scores, coupled with other pertinent facts, the instructor presents and explains the

ENGLISH

	CLOZE SCORES	< 44%	44 - 57%	> 57%
MOTHER TONGUE	< 44%	(1) LEARNER	(2) ESL	(3) ESL
	44 - 57%	(4) ESL	(5) LEARNER	(6) ESL
	> 57%	(7) ESL	(8) ESL	(9) LEARNER

Figure 3. Choice Alternatives Resulting from Diagnosis with the Cloze Procedure

adult's instructional alternatives: cloze scores of less than 44 percent suggest a frustration level, cloze scores of 44-57 percent suggest instructional level, and cloze scores of more than 57 percent suggest independent level.

Recommendations following cloze tests are shown in Figure 3.

Cells 1, 5, 9 = Alternative 1, learner's choice; bilingual balance exists as a negative of positive condition. As a negative condition (Cell 1), bilingual balance is a literacy deficit in both languages. As a positive condition, Cell 5 suggests a balanced instructional level; and Cell 9 indicates an independent operating level in both languages.

Cells 4, 7, 8 = Alternative 2, primary instruction in the vernacular; English is taught as a second language.

Cells 2, 3, 4 = Alternative 3, primary instruction in English; second language instruction is given.

The learner is central to all decisions. No matter what other students are doing, the individual adult will ultimately decide what, when, how much, and in what language his own literacy training will take place. Through a continuous renewal process (Task V), the adult learner is guided toward a positive bicultural, bilingual condition.

Feedforward (in Figure 2) is comprised of the adult's learning activities formulated as a prescriptive program. Acting in a colaborative and consultative capacity, the instructor selects materials, learning settings, teaching methods, and estimates the time that the learner may need to master his objectives. In pacing the adult learner's potential, the Learning Rate Test (6) could be used.

During *implementation* the learner is exposed to a well-planned program that is a live, dynamic, vital succession of enabling skills. The program brings about changes for the better in both the individual and the society in which he lives. The instructor maintains a partnership role in helping the adult learner to find out what is "the better." *Feedback* gives the learner a knowledge of the results of his efforts. Self-evaluation and program modification are facilitated, as needed. Through *reinforcement* each learner is provided with educational experiences which will strengthen and extend his newly acquired skills.

Mastery-measurement provides the learner with instruments appropriate for achievement measurement. He is guided in the analysis to determine whether he is ready to go on to new work, or requires additional sequences to accommodate deficits.

Task V: Provision for Continuous Organizational Renewal

As any organization is comprised of people, so is the bilingual adult education program an organization made up of the human side of enterprise. Therefore, the bilingual system must make provision for a continuous process of organizational renewal. Lippitt (*12*:1) defines *organizational renewal* as "the process of initiating, creating, and confronting needed changes so as to make it possible for organizations to become or remain viable, to adapt to new conditions, to solve problems, to learn from experiences, and to move toward greater organizational maturity."

The renewal process (Figure 2) is more than measurement and evaluation. It is an ongoing linkage of appropriate human resources to achieve desired results. It is the constant effort to deal with problems that arise as mature learners come face-to-face with realities of the present. It is understanding the adult learner as a human resource molded mainly by his experiential past. It is approaching in an efficient, effective, and humane way the behavioral changes that must take place as learners confront realistically the situations with which they must cope. The renewal process can be summarized in the following eight steps.

1. The adult comes from the external environment to enter the bilingual education system. He becomes a human resource who contributes to organization objectives.
2. Through procedures already discussed, the literacy imperatives of the adult learner are identified. Subject matter and related concepts are separated for analysis and curriculum planning.
3. Cloze procedure and other tools of assessment are utilized in establishing language levels in the vernacular and English.
4. Diagnostic techniques are used to give the adult learner guidance and counselling that enable him to establish his language preferences. No pressures are imposed on him to follow one alternative or another.
5. Based on his literacy imperative, a prescriptive program is formulated for the learner. Objectives are those that he has identified; the instructor acts in a consultative and collaborative capacity.
6. The program is implemented. All human resources in the bilingual education system are linked to accomplish organizational objectives. A continuous diagnostic procedure is employed to facilitate changes needed to accommodate language alterations that take place.

Adult Literacy Programs

7. Measurement and evaluation are ongoing processes. When the learner has fulfilled a prescription, an assessment is made to determine whether he has accomplished his objectives, or whether he must be exposed to additional instructional segments.

8. If the learner's objectives have not been met, he is returned to the station that prepares prescriptions. He receives a revised set of learning activities that include only unmet objectives. If his objectives have been met, he is recycled to the interview station where other imperatives for language learning are determined.

Discussion

The ABC Model conceptualizes the adult learner, not as a kind of stimulus-response machine vending (*18*), but as an electronic computer fashioned after Guilford's Structure of Intellect (*8*). The computer is fed information; it stores the information, uses it to generate new information by either divergent or convergent thinking, and evaluates its own results. The adult learner has a unique feature not shared by his mechanical counterpart. The human can utilize the contents of his storage bank by going beyond the computer to seek and discover new information outside himself. The adult is led to the notion that learning is the discovery of information, not merely the formation of associations.

The program proposed in this paper operates under the assumption that the true literacy program for adults can be found where the instructor meets the learner, and not within the covers of a printed guide or published textbook. The adult educator who employs a packaged prescription, without modification or adaptation to meet the needs, interests, and abilities of the learner, is merely dramatizing experiences which may have been real to some adult, but which are outside the range of reality for the learner at hand.

In the ABC Model, learning operations begin with the perception of self-needs and possibilities. The adult learner is guided to expand and increase his abilities to perceive, using his whole environment of past and present experiences and resources. He gains competence in handling external objects and operations of living in an English dominant world through more perceiving, structuring, evaluating, imagining, synthesizing, creating, and transforming.

He undergoes all types of experiences that help him to develop communication skills in the vernacular and in English. He acts as the gatekeeper of the quality and quantity of his learning activities, guided and directed by the school. In this capacity, he can modify or accept segments of cultural differences to which he is exposed. He can reject acculturation he perceives as incompatible with his primary value system. He holds the key to his literacy training.

The adult learns how to learn and, in doing so, frees his mind. He becomes a member of the learning society in an effective, efficient, and humane way. The ABC Model helps adult educators to define biculturalism for a particular community, so that appropriate programs may be designed for the local learning society.

The adult learner and the community are linked to create an integrated learning system that helps the individual to improve his communication skills. The adult learns how to learn and, in doing so, functions as the gatekeeper of the method and material to which he is exposed. He possesses enabling skills that help him to operate with equal effectiveness in a bicultural, bilingual society.

REFERENCES

1. Andersson, Theodore, and Mildred Andersson. *Bilingual Schooling in the United States.* Austin, Texas: Southwest Educational Development Laboratory, 1970.
2. Appelson, Marilyn, and Barry F. Semple. *English and Citizenship Programs for the Foreign Born: A Handbook for Teachers.* Trenton: New Jersey State Department of Education, 1971.
3. Bilingual Education Act, Title VII, ESEA.
4. "Bilingual Monthly," *Saturday Review of Education,* 1 (March 10, 1973), 63.
5. Brennan, Pamela, and Anna Acitelli Donoghue. *Biculturalism Through Experiential Language Learning.* San Diego, California: San Diego Community College, 1972.
6. Durrell, Donald. *Improving Reading Instruction.* New York: Harcourt, 1956.
7. *ESEA Title VII Project Summary, By State and Project Location Giving Grant Award and Cumulative Total.* Washington, D.C.: Undated.
8. Guilford, J. P. "Three Faces of Intellect," *American Psychologist,* 14 (1959), 469-479.
9. Gutierrez, Medardo. *Bilingualism and Bilingual Education Programs.* Albany, New York: State University of New York, 1972.
10. Hutchins, Robert M. *The Learning Society.* New York: Praeger, 1968.
11. Leagans, J. Paul. "A Concept of Needs," *Journal of Cooperative Extension,* 2 (Summer 1964), 89-96.
12. Lippitt, Gordon L. *Organizational Renewal.* New York: Appleton-Century-Crofts, 1969.
13. Massoglia, Elinor T. "Literacy Imperatives in Adult Education," unpublished manuscript, 1970.
14. Massoglia, Elinor T. "Cloze Procedure as a Predictor of Course Grade-Point Average of Graduate Students Enrolled in a Course in Adult Education," doctoral dissertation, North Carolina State University, 1971.

15. *Manual for Project Applicants and Grantees.* Bilingual Education Act, Title VII, ESEA. Washington, D.C.: U.S. Department of Health, Education, and Welfare, April 20, 1971.

16. Politzer, Robert L. "The Foreign Language Curriculum: Present Problems," *School and Society*, January 1972, 15-19.

17. Prosser, Roy. "Research in Adult Education," in Lars-Olof Edstrom et al. (Eds.), *Mass Education.* Stockholm: The Dag Hammarskjold Foundation, 1970, 88.

18. Skinner, B. F. *The Behavior of Organisms.* New York: Macmillan, 1953.

19. Taylor, Wilson L. "Cloze Procedure: A New Tool for Measuring Readability," *Journalism Quarterly,* 30 (Fall 1953), 414-438.

20. Tyler, Ralph W. *Basic Principles of Curriculum and Instruction.* Chicago: The University of Chicago Press, 1950.

21. Wissot, Jay. "A Total Approach to the High School English-as-a-Second-Language Program," *TESOL QUARTERLY,* Vol. 4, No. 3 (September 1970), 361-364.

☐ Atkinson, L. "Black College Reading Teachers' Dual Role," *Journal of Reading,* 16 (May 1973), 612-621.

☐ Bochtler, S. "Reading Goes to Jail – and Sends a Word to All," *Journal of Reading,* 17 (April 1974), 527-530.

☐ Bormuth, J. "Reading Literacy: Its Definition and Assessment," *Reading Research Quarterly,* 9 (1973-1974), 7-66.

☐ Brown, D. "Measuring the Reading Ability and Potential of Adult Illiterates," in R. Farr (Ed.), *Measurement and Evaluation of Reading.* New York: Harcourt, 1970, 154-165.

☐ Brown, D., and A. Newman. "Research in Adult Literacy," *Journal of Reading Behavior,* 2 (Winter 1970), 19-46.

☐ Evans, H., and E. DuBois. "Community/Junior College Remedial Programs – Reflections," *Journal of Reading,* 16 (October 1972), 38-45.

☐ Green, F. (Ed.). *College Reading: Problems and Programs of Junior and Senior Colleges,* Twenty-First Yearbook of the National Reading Conference, Volume II. Boone, North Carolina: National Reading Conference, 1972.

☐ Johns, J. "A List of Basic Sight Words for Older Disabled Readers," *English Journal,* 61 (October 1972), 1057-1059.

☐ Kelly, L. "Survival Literacy: Teaching Reading to Those with a 'Need to Know,'" *Journal of Reading,* 17 (February 1974), 352-355.

☐ Manzo, A. "Teaching Adults to Read," in P. Nacke (Ed.), *Diversity in Mature Reading: Theory and Research,* Twenty-Second Yearbook of the National Reading Conference, Volume 1. Boone, North Carolina: National Reading Conference, 1973, 190-198.

☐ Nacke, P. (Ed.). *Programs and Practices for College Reading,* Twenty-Second Yearbook of the National Reading Conference, Volume II. Boone, North Carolina: National Reading Conference, 1973.

☐ O'Donnell, M. "Reading for the Untaught – Working With Adult Illiterates," *Journal of Reading,* 17 (October 1973), 32-35.

☐ Olsen, T. "International Adult Education," *Journal of Reading,* 16 (April 1973), 584-589.

☐ Rankin, E. "A Simple Model for the Improvement of College-Training for Reading Development," in P. Nacke (Ed.), *Diversity in Mature Reading: Theory and Research,* Twenty-Second Yearbook of the National Reading Conference, Volume 1. Boone, North Carolina: National Reading Conference, 1973, 1-10.